BECOMING A LEADER AFTER GOD'S HEART

A Study of 1 & 2 Samuel and 1 Chronicles

Jack W. Hayford
with
Joseph Snider

THOMAS NELSON PUBLISHERS
Nashville

Becoming a Leader After God's Heart
A Study of 1 & 2 Samuel and 1 Chronicles
Copyright © 1997 by Jack W. Hayford

Published in Nashville, Tennessee, by Thomas Nelson, Inc.

Unless otherwise indicated, Scripture quotations are from the *New King James Version* of the Bible, © 1979, 1980, 1982, Thomas Nelson, Inc., Publishers

Printed in the United States of America
1 2 3 4 5 6 7 8 — 03 02 01 00 99 98

CONTENTS

Becoming a Leader After God's Heart (A Study of 1 & 2 Samuel and 1 Chronicles) is one of a series of study guides that focus exciting, discovery-geared coverage of Bible book and power themes—all prompting toward dynamic, Holy Spirit-filled living.

About the Executive Editor

JACK W. HAYFORD, noted pastor, teacher, writer, and composer, is the Executive Editor of the complete series, working with the publisher in the conceiving and developing of each of the books.

Dr. Hayford is Senior Pastor of The Church On The Way, the First Foursquare Church of Van Nuys, California. He and his wife, Anna, have four married children, all of whom are active in either pastoral ministry or vital church life. As General Editor of the *Spirit-Filled Life® Bible*, Pastor Hayford led a four-year project, which has resulted in the availability of one of today's most practical and popular study Bibles. He is author of more than twenty books, including *A Passion for Fullness, The Beauty of Spiritual Language, Rebuilding the Real You,* and *Prayer Is Invading the Impossible*. His musical compositions number over four hundred songs, including the widely sung "Majesty."

About the Writer

JOSEPH SNIDER is director of family ministries for Fellowship Missionary Church in Fort Wayne, Indiana. His knowledge of the Bible has been sharpened through experience as a youth evangelist with Young Life in Dallas, a faculty member of Fort Wayne Bible College (now Taylor University, Fort Wayne), and three pastoral positions in Indiana in addition to several years of freelance writing.

Married to Sally Snider, Joe has two grown children, Jenny and Ted. They live in Indianapolis, Indiana. Joe earned a B.A. in English from Cedarville College in Cedarville, Ohio, and a Th.M. in Christian Education from Dallas Theological Seminary.

Of this contributor, the General Editor has remarked: "Joe Snider's strength and stability as a gracious, godly man comes through in his writing. His perceptive and practical way of pointing the way to truth inspires students of God's Word."

THE GIFT
THAT KEEPS ON GIVING

One of the most precious gifts God has given us is His Word, the Bible. Wrapped in the glory and sacrifice of His Son and delivered by the power and ministry of His Spirit, it is a treasured gift—the gift that keeps on giving, because the Giver it reveals is inexhaustible in His love and grace.

Tragically, though, fewer and fewer people are opening this gift and seeking to understand what it's all about and how to use it. They often feel intimidated by it. It requires some assembly, and its instructions are hard to comprehend sometimes. How does the Bible fit together anyway? What does this ancient Book have to say to us who are looking toward the twenty-first century? Will taking the time and energy to understand its instructions and to fit it all together really help you and me?

Yes. Yes. Without a shred of doubt.

The *Spirit-Filled Life® Bible Discovery Guide* series is designed to help you unwrap, assemble, and enjoy all God has for you in the pages of Scripture. It will focus your time and energy on the books of the Bible, the people and places they describe, and the themes and life applications that flow thick from its pages like honey oozing from a beehive.

So you can get the most out of God's Word, this series has a number of helpful features:

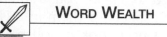

WORD WEALTH

"WORD WEALTH" provides definitions of key terms.

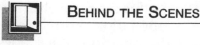

BEHIND THE SCENES

"BEHIND THE SCENES" supplies information about cultural practices, doctrinal disputes, business trades, etc.

AT A GLANCE

"AT A GLANCE" feature—helpful maps and charts.

 BIBLE EXTRA

"BIBLE EXTRA" will guide you to other resources that will enable you to glean more from the Bible's wealth.

PROBING THE DEPTHS

"PROBING THE DEPTHS," will explain controversial issues raised by particular lessons and cite Bible passages and other sources to help you come to your own conclusions.

 FAITH ALIVE

The "FAITH ALIVE" feature will help you see and apply the Bible to your day-to-day needs.

As you'll see, these guides supply space for you to answer the study and life-application questions and exercises. You may, however, want to record all your answers, or just the overflow from your study or application, in a separate notebook or journal. This would be especially helpful if you think you'll dig into the BIBLE EXTRA features. Because the exercises in this feature are optional and can be expanded as far as you want to take them, we have not allowed writing space for them in this study guide. So you may want to have a notebook or journal handy for recording your discoveries while working through to this feature's riches.

The Bible study method used in this series revolves around four basic steps: observation, interpretation, correlation, and application. Observation answers the question, What does the text say? Interpretation deals with, What does the text mean?— not with what it means to you or me, but what it meant to its original readers. Correlation asks, What light do other Scripture passages shed on this text? And application, the goal of Bible study, poses the question, How should my life change in response to the Holy Spirit's teaching of this text?

If you have used a Bible much before, you know that it comes in a variety of translations and paraphrases. Although you can use any of them with profit as you work through the *Spirit-Filled Life*® *Bible Discovery Guide* series, when Bible passages or words are cited, you will find they are from the New King James Version of the Bible. Using this translation with this series will make your study easier, but it's certainly not necessary.

The only resources you need to complete and apply these study guides are a heart and mind open to the Holy Spirit, a prayerful attitude, and a pencil and a Bible. Of course, you may draw upon other sources, but these study guides are comprehensive enough to give you all you need to gain a good, basic understanding of the Bible book being covered and how you can apply its themes and counsel to your life.

A word of warning, though. By itself, Bible study will not transform your life. It will not give you power, peace, joy, comfort, hope, and a number of other gifts God longs for you to unwrap and enjoy. Through Bible study, you will grow in your understanding of the Lord, His kingdom and your place in it, but you must be sure to rely on the Holy Spirit to guide your study and your application of the Bible's truths. He, Jesus promises, was sent to teach us "all things" (John 14:26; cf. 1 Cor. 2:13). Bathe your study time in prayer, asking the Spirit of God to illuminate the text, enlighten your mind, humble your will, and comfort your heart. He will never let you down.

My prayer and goal for you is that as you unwrap and begin to explore God's Book for living His way, the Holy Spirit will fill every fiber of your being with the joy and power God longs to give all His children. So read on. Be diligent. Stay open and submissive to Him. You will not be disappointed. He promises you!

Samuel:
Listening to the Voice of God
1 Samuel 1—12

Lesson 1 / A Dedicated Life

1 Samuel 1:1—4:1a;
1 Chronicles 6:1–48

In the early days of the 20th century, a Mennonite woman living in the Amish country of northern Indiana gave birth to a son. In a dream the Lord told this devout mother that her son would grow up to become a preacher. So she named the infant boy Herald.

Herald grew up hearing over and over the story of his common name with the uncommon spelling. He resented his name and he resented that his mother had decided in advance what he should do with his life. On the outside Herald was a model son who faithfully attended the rural Mennonite church with his family, but inside he was determined to be anything but a herald.

Herald could resist his mother who told the story of his naming but not the Lord who had given her the prophecy. He became a pastor whose compassionate heart drew many to follow Christ. Herald married a woman named Miriam, a perfect match for him in spirit and in ministry.

Samuel's mother could have named her son Herald too. The child Samuel grew to be a prophet (1 Sam. 3:20), and a prophet is a "herald" of God's Word. Interestingly the Miriam in the Old Testament—Moses' sister—also was a prophetess (Ex. 15:20).

THE BIG PICTURE

The Books of 1 and 2 Samuel tell the stories of three main

individuals. Together their lives and careers span the transition from the judges to the kings of Israel. After nine chapters of genealogies, 1 Chronicles covers the same time frame (plus a little) as 2 Samuel.

Identify the three main characters of these books, along with their occupations.

CHARACTER   **OCCUPATIONS**

1. _____   _____

   (1 Sam. 1:20)   (3:20; 7:15)

2. _____   _____

   (1 Sam. 9:2)   (10:17–24)

3. _____   _____

   (1 Sam. 16:11–13)   (2 Sam. 5:1–5)

AT A GLANCE[1]

ISRAEL BEFORE DAVID BECAME KING

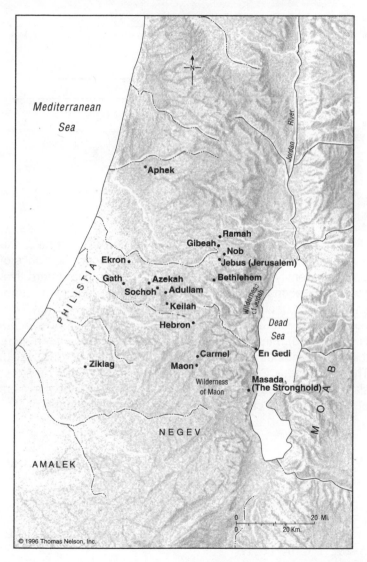

Write the names of the hometowns of Samuel, Saul, and David below and underline them on the map above.

- Samuel (1 Sam. 2:11) _____

- Saul (1 Sam. 10:26) _____

- David (1 Sam. 17:12–15) _____

BEHIND THE SCENES

The books of Samuel carry his name because he is the first main character in them. They could be called the books of David to identify the main character of the combined narrative. First and Second Samuel were written by an unknown author after David's death (2 Sam. 23:1) and perhaps after the kingdom divided into Judah and Israel following Solomon's death (1 Sam. 27:6). First and Second Chronicles were written more than five centuries after the lives of Samuel, Saul, and David. The anonymous Chronicler compiled a second history emphasizing genealogies and official records that helped the survivors of the Babylonian captivity reconnect themselves to the past.

What is the great task that Samuel carries out for the Lord in these books of the Bible? (1 Sam. 9:15–17; 10:1; 16:1–13)

What is Saul remembered for from these books? (1 Sam. 15:17–29; 1 Chr. 10:13)

What is David's primary role in the unfolding story of the quest for God's king? (2 Sam. 7:4, 8–12; 1 Chr. 17:7, 11)

What are some of the notable actions of the Holy Spirit in these books?

• 1 Samuel 10:1, 6–10

• 1 Samuel 11:6, 7

• 1 Samuel 16:1, 13

• 1 Samuel 16:14–16

• 1 Samuel 19:18–24

• 1 Chronicles 12:16–18

• 1 Chronicles 28:10–12

• 2 Samuel 23:1–3

A GIFT THAT KEEPS GIVING

The search for God's king to rule for Him over His people Israel began in an obscure hill country village with the distress of a barren woman who wanted a child. Her faith, her prayer, her resolute vow to give her son back to the Lord served as the launchpad for the kingdom of Israel and all it pictured of the kingdom of God in Christ.

What can you observe from the opening verses of 1 Samuel

about Samuel's father Elkanah? (1 Sam. 1:1–3; 1 Chr. 6:26–28)

Describe the worship arrangements for Israel at the end of the period of the judges when Samuel was born.

• The location of the tabernacle and ark of the covenant (1 Sam. 1:3)

• The priests who offered sacrifices for worshipers (1 Sam. 1:3)

• How the worshipers participated in thank offerings to the Lord (1 Sam. 1:4)

BIBLE EXTRA

Joshua temporarily pitched the tabernacle at Gilgal while Israel defeated Jericho and conquered the rest of Canaan (Josh. 4:19). After the conquest, the tabernacle was moved permanently to Shiloh at the heart of Israelite territory (18:1). All through the period of the judges—more than three hundred years (Judg. 11:26)—Shiloh was the center of Israel's worship. When the Philistines captured the ark in battle (1 Sam. 4:10,11), they apparently destroyed Shiloh and disrupted tabernacle worship in Israel so brutally that the calamity was never forgotten (see Ps. 78:60–64; Jer. 7:12; 26:6).

What can you discover or infer from these verses about the personality and character of these people? (1 Sam. 1:4–11)

• Elkanah

• Peninnah

• Hannah

What do you conclude about the faith of Hannah from each of these?

• The future she envisioned for her son (1 Sam 1:11)

• Her concern about Eli's opinion of her (1 Sam. 1:14–16)

• The encouragement she drew from the priest's blessing (1 Sam. 1:17, 18)

BEHIND THE SCENES

Hannah promised the Lord that if He gave her a son she would raise him as a Nazirite. A Nazirite was one who consecrated himself to holy living and showed that by refraining from alcohol, contact with the dead, and haircuts or shaves (Num. 6:1–21). Samson was a Nazirite (Judg. 13:5) who failed to live up to his commitments. Samuel lived all his life in conformity to his mother's vow (1 Sam. 12:1–5).

What do you think was meant by Hannah's prayer that the Lord would "remember" her (1 Sam. 1:11) and the answer in which He "remembered" her (v. 19)? Had the Lord forgotten her or ignored her before?

Why do you think Hannah is portrayed as being in charge of choosing the time when Samuel went to Shiloh, the offering given for him, and his presentation to Eli? (1 Sam. 1:21–28)

What do you think it meant to Hannah to give her son to the Lord and for Samuel to remain at Shiloh and serve the Lord there as an assistant to the priests? (1 Sam. 1:11, 28)

Hannah's prayer was a prophetic utterance inspired by the Spirit of God. Mary the mother of Jesus relied on its ideas when she praised the Lord with her cousin Elizabeth as they reflected on their miracle pregnancies (Luke 1:46–55). What does Hannah's prayer reveal about these subjects?

• How to rely on the Lord (1 Sam. 2:1–3)

• How God works among people (1 Sam. 2:4–8a)

• How the power of God operates (1 Sam. 2:8b–10)

What was Hannah's Spirit-given prophecy at the end of verse 10 that sets the stage for the rest of 1 and 2 Samuel?

WORD WEALTH

Hannah rejoiced in God's **salvation** (1 Sam. 2:1). The Hebrew word contains the literal idea of width in contrast to narrowness and the figurative sense of freedom in contrast to distress. Hannah had been distressed by her barrenness. It restricted and oppressed her every waking moment. The Lord gave her liberty and joy through a son. The ultimate restriction and distress in life is separation from God caused by sin. God has provided the sacrifice through the death of Jesus that liberates all who receive His salvation through faith. The Hebrew term translated **salvation** appears in the biblical names Joshua, Hosea, Isaiah, and Jesus (Yeshua).

 FAITH ALIVE

How can we dedicate our children to the Lord and raise them to realize that we nurture them in order to give them back to God as His servants?

A GIFT OF WORSHIP

The boy Samuel moved from a godly home at Ramah in which his mother and father were scrupulous in their worship of the Lord to the priestly home of Eli at Shiloh in which the worship of the Lord was scorned. Would Samuel be corrupted by Eli's sons with whom he worked? Would Samuel be a good influence on the older sons of Eli? What was Eli's attitude and response to his sons and to Samuel?

What is the initial quick contrast between Samuel and the priestly sons of Eli? (1 Sam. 2:11, 12)

The Law of Moses prescribed that certain portions of offerings should go to the priests (Lev. 7:34; Deut. 18:3). But the priest was to burn the fat of the offering—representing the best—before he took his portion (Lev. 7:29–31). How did the sons of Eli violate God's priestly regulations? (1 Sam. 2:13–16)

What was the effect of the sins of Eli's sons on Israelite worshipers? (1 Sam. 2:17)

How did Hannah maintain her connection to Samuel as he grew up at Shiloh? (1 Sam. 2:18, 19)

How did Eli respond to Samuel's parents at their annual visits? (1 Sam. 2:20)

How did the Lord bless Hannah for her faithfulness? (1 Sam. 2:21)

What was the last straw in his sons' behavior that moved Eli to rebuke them? (1 Sam. 2:22)

What did Eli tell his sons in an attempt to correct their sinful behavior? (1 Sam. 2:23–25)

At this point in the narrative, contrast the attitude of God toward Eli's sons and toward Samuel. (1 Sam. 2:25b, 26)

What did the anonymous prophet of God announce to Eli about the past, present, and future of his priestly family? (1 Sam. 2:27–36)

 BIBLE EXTRA

In an immediate sense, Samuel became the faithful priest more approved than Eli's family. In the long run, Eli's descendants continued to serve a trouble-plagued priesthood about eighty years more until Abiathar was replaced by Zadok, who ministered during the reign of Solomon (1 Kin. 2:27). Abiathar unwisely backed David's son Adonijah in his abortive attempt to succeed David as king (1:7, 8).

 FAITH ALIVE

Elkanah, Hannah, and even Eli helped protect Samuel from the evil influences of Eli's sons. Who in your life functions as spiritual guards and guides to help you follow the Lord?

What ministry to the body of Christ or the world has God protected you through these people to perform?

A GIFT OF PROPHECY

While Samuel grew and flourished as an assistant priest to Eli, he had no idea that God had a much greater role in mind for him. Samuel would prove to be the great transitional figure from the time of the judges to the Davidic monarchy. To do that, Samuel had to become a prophetic spokesman for the Lord. Only as a prophet could he function as kingmaker and conscience of Israel.

What was the prophetic climate like as Samuel grew up at the tabernacle in Shiloh? (1 Sam. 3:1)

Describe the process by which Samuel first heard a prophetic word from the Lord. (1 Sam. 3:2–10)

Why did Samuel need the spiritual guidance of the older man Eli? (1 Sam. 3:7–9)

Neither the sons of Eli nor Samuel could be said to "know the LORD" (1 Sam. 2:12; 3:7). What was the difference in their spiritual "ignorance" at this time?

What was the first prophetic message the Lord revealed to Samuel? (1 Sam. 3:11–14)

Describe these responses after Samuel received his first prophecy.

• Samuel's response to the situation (1 Sam. 3:15)

• Samuel's response to Eli's direct order (1 Sam. 3:16–18a)

• Eli's response to God's prophecy through Samuel (1 Sam. 3:18b)

Why did word spread throughout Israel that there was a prophet once again at Shiloh? (1 Sam. 3:19–21)

WORD WEALTH

A **prophet** is someone who announces a message at the direction of the Lord God. **Prophet** translates the Hebrew word *nabi'*, which means a herald, a spokesman, or an announcer. *Nabi'* occurs more than three hundred times in the Old Testament. Six times the word is feminine, referring to Miriam (Ex. 15:20), Deborah (Judg. 4:4), Huldah (2 Kin. 22:14; 2 Chr. 34:22), Noadiah (Neh. 6:14), and Isaiah's wife (Is. 8:3). The word can refer to false prophets of false gods (Deut. 13:1–3), but nearly always refers to the Lord's commissioned spokes-people.[2]

 KINGDOM EXTRA

Samuel is an example of the "office" of the "prophet" in the Old Testament. This role differs from the operation of the gift of prophecy in the life of the believer, for it entails a Christ-appointed ministry of a person rather than the Holy Spirit-distributed gift *through* a person.

In the New Testament, the incident of Agabus (Acts 11:27–30) resulted in effective action by the church's rising to meet a challenging situation. This is a valid test of the prophetic office. The prophetic office is for edification and not for enter-tainment—to enlarge and refresh the body, whether locally or beyond.

Nothing in the New Testament reduces the stringent requirements for serving this role, and Deuteronomy 18:20–22 ought to be regarded seriously. Prophecy is nothing to be "experimented" with, for souls are in the balance in the exercise of every ministry.[3]

FAITH ALIVE

One of the results of the New Testament outpouring of the Holy Spirit is the broadening of God's prophetic communication. In Old Testament times only a select few received such words from the Lord. In the age of the Spirit begun by Jesus, all be-lievers—men and women, old and young—may expect God to speak to them in order to minister to others (Acts 2:16–18; 1 Cor. 14; Col. 3:16; 1 Thess. 5:20, 21).

Describe any experience in which you believe God spoke to you about a specific situation.

Samuel needed the experience of Eli to understand God was speaking to him. How can the leaders of your church help you discern when you believe God is speaking to you?

1. *Spirit-Filled Life® Bible* (Nashville: Thomas Nelson Publishers, 1991), 427, map of "Before David Became King."
2. Ibid., 401, "Word Wealth: 1 Sam. 3:20, prophet."
3. Ibid., 1647, "Kingdom Dynamics: Acts 11:27–30, The Office of the Prophet."

Lesson 2/A Time of Great Need
1 Samuel 4:1b—7:17

Winston Churchill rose to prominence as one of Britain's leading military strategists and political stars in the early years of the twentieth century. Then during World War I he backed a campaign in Turkey that failed miserably. He was blamed and confided to a friend, "I am finished."

Churchill remained in Parliament and cabinet posts, but he became an invisible man in the period between the World Wars. He devoted himself to historical writing and to painting and excelled at both. He opposed Prime Minister Neville Chamberlain's diplomatic policy toward Adolf Hitler and the National Socialists. Churchill called it appeasement.

Many were astounded when, after twenty years of relative obscurity, Churchill was asked to form a new government and lead Britain through the war he and few others had foreseen as inevitable. He was sixty-six years old. Through the course of World War II, Winston Churchill embodied the British bulldog spirit of determination.

Similarly Samuel dominates the first three chapters of 1 Samuel and then fades into the background while the spiritual and political affairs of Israel deteriorates. Then in Israel's darkest hour, Samuel emerges again as an older, wiser man to serve as God's instrument of deliverance.

GOD CLEANS HOUSE

Although God elevated Samuel in the esteem of Israel as a priest at Shiloh and as a prophet, the spiritual level of the nation was sinking to the level of Eli's sons. Before Samuel could have his true impact on Israel, judgment would have "to begin at the house of God" (1 Pet. 4:17).

AT A GLANCE

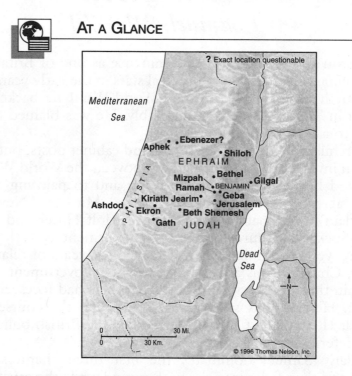

The Ministry of Samuel. As judge, Samuel visited yearly the cities of Bethel, Gilgal, and Mizpah.[1]

What event marked the beginning of Israel's spiritual and political problems? (1 Sam. 4:1b, 2)

What solution to their problems did the elders of Israel propose? (1 Sam. 4:3, 4)

How did the opposing armies react to the presence of the ark in Israel's camp?

• Israel's army (1 Sam. 4:5)

• The Philistine army (1 Sam. 4:6–9)

 WORD WEALTH

The Hebrew word translated **shout** indicates a shout of joy, jubilation, or victory. *Teru'ah* is an ear-piercing, great noise; a sound that cannot be ignored. This kind of shout brought down the walls of Jericho (Josh. 6:5). This kind of joyful noise would welcome the ark back to Israel (2 Sam. 6:15). While the earth shook when the Israelite army shouted (1 Sam. 4:5), and the Philistines were inclined to quake as well, this was a shout of presumption rather than a shout of faith.[2]

How did the opposing armies fare in the battle that followed the arrival of the ark in the Israelite camp? (1 Sam. 4:10, 11)

• The frightened Philistines

• The confident Israelites

A Benjamite messenger ran the twenty miles from Aphek uphill to Shiloh in less than a day (1 Sam. 4:12). How did each of these respond to his terrible news of the defeat of Israel and the capture of the ark of the covenant?

- The town of Shiloh (1 Sam. 4:13)

- Eli (1 Sam. 4:13–18)

- Eli's daughter-in-law, Phinehas' wife (1 Sam. 4:19–22)

WORD WEALTH

Glory literally meant weightiness or substantialness. By extension it came to mean wealth and then the honor and influence that goes along with prominence. When applied to God, **glory** means honor and majesty, with a special emphasis on His visual splendor or radiance that appeared on Mount Sinai (Ex. 19:16), led the Israelites through the wilderness (Num. 9:15–23), and filled the temple at its dedication (1 Kin. 8:10, 11). Two biblical names contain this word: Jochebed ("Yahweh Is Glory") and Ichabod ("Where Is the Glory?").[3]

At the end of his life, how did Eli's physical condition reflect the problems of his spiritual life?

In 1 Samuel 4:10–22, underline all the occurrences of the phrases "the ark of God was captured" and "the ark of God has been captured." How many times do these expressions occur in these verses? _____ How do the responses of Shiloh, Eli, and Phinehas's wife to this event underline the depth of tragedy they sensed?

FAITH ALIVE

What do you think would be your response if you were cut off from the presence of the Lord?

Write a brief prayer of gratitude that the Lord will never leave you or forsake you.

GOD COMES HOME TO ISRAEL

Israel could not manipulate God by means of His ark to give them victory when their hearts weren't right before Him. Certainly the pagan Philistines could not manipulate the Lord for their ends by possessing the ark of the covenant. The real ark gave the real Philistines as much real trouble as the fictional ark gave the fictional Nazis in the fictional *Raiders of the Lost Ark*.

What happened when the Philistines put the captured ark of the covenant in the temple of their chief deity Dagon? (1 Sam. 5:1–5)

BEHIND THE SCENES

Among the Canaanite gods, El was the greatest, but the Canaanites did not pay much attention to him. The fertility god Baal was the favorite of most native peoples of Canaan. The immigrant Philistines, however, favored Dagon, the father of Baal. Dagon was a god of grain.

The hands of Dagon were powerless before the living God of Israel. Read 1 Samuel 5:6—6:9 and underline every reference to the hand of the Lord. How many did you find? _____

What must the Philistines have concluded about the hand of the Lord?

What happened in Ashdod, Gath, and Ekron (refer to earlier map) because the Philistines tried to hold "the ark of the covenant of the LORD of hosts who dwells between the cherubim" (1 Sam. 4:4) captive? (1 Sam. 5:6–12)

 ## BEHIND THE SCENES

Because the tumors of this plague on the Philistines are associated in some way with rats (1 Sam. 6:4), many commentators identify the tumors as the swellings known as buboes that give their name to bubonic plague. If so, this is the earliest recorded case of bubonic plague and may be when it made its deadly entrance into human history.[4]

How did the Philistines formulate their plan for dealing with the ark of the Lord? (1 Sam. 6:1, 2)

What was the scheme that the priests and diviners suggested to the Philistines? (1 Sam. 6:3–9)

Why do you think the Philistines were so mindful of how the Egyptians had mishandled their conflict with the God of Israel? (1 Sam. 6:6; see 4:6, 7)

What role did each of these play in the return of the ark of the Lord to Israelite territory? (1 Sam. 6:10–16)

• The two milk cows who had never been separated from their calves

• The five Philistines lords

• The residents of Beth Shemesh

 BEHIND THE SCENES

Beth Shemesh lay about nine miles east southeast of Ekron. The name **Beth Shemesh** meant "The House of the Sun" and probably had earlier been a center of Canaanite sun worship.[5] The town lay within the tribal territory of Judah, but Joshua had designated it as a Levitical city (Josh. 21:16). That explains the presence of Levites to transport the ark and offer sacrifices when the milk cows delivered it unexpectedly (1 Sam. 6:15).

How was the land of Philistia organized and governed? How did this structure influence the way the Philistines returned the ark of the Lord? (1 Sam. 6:17, 18)

Why did the residents of Beth Shemesh refuse to let the ark of the Lord remain in their community? (1 Sam. 6:19, 20)

What arrangements were made for the housing and service of the ark until a permanent site could be provided at a later date? (1 Sam. 6:21—7:1)

BEHIND THE SCENES

The number 50,070 is much larger than the population of Beth Shemesh would have been. Hebrew numbers were written in words rather than a system of numeric symbols. In several places in the Old Testament it appears that ancient scribes had difficulty transmitting these awkward numeric phrases exactly. This is one of the most puzzling. Some modern versions arbitrarily keep the number 70 and translate the rest of the phrase differently or disregard it. There doesn't seem to be a convincing solution at this time.[6]

FAITH ALIVE

What are some ways in which you think unbelievers try to "use" God for their own ends?

What do you think happens to people who use God's name but have no connection to His power through a relationship with Jesus Christ?

How do you think we can demonstrate to the world that the Lord is at home among us?

ISRAEL COMES HOME TO GOD

The ark of the covenant had returned to Israel, but Israel was no more ready to serve the Lord than they had been when the ark was captured. Shiloh and its worship center apparently had been destroyed by the Philistines after the battle at Aphek (see Ps. 78:60–64; Jer. 7:12; 26:6). The time was ripe for the Lord to do something through Samuel whom He had prepared for just such a time.

Describe Israel's problem and its solution as the Lord worked through Samuel.

- The problem (1 Sam. 7:2)

- The proposed solution (1 Sam. 7:3

- The response to the proposed solution (1 Sam. 7:4)

Samuel arranged a formal ceremony to seal the national repentance of Israel. What did each do there? (1 Sam. 7:5, 6)

- Samuel

- Israel

 WORD WEALTH

When Samuel promised to **pray** for Israel (1 Sam. 7:5), he was promising to intercede on their behalf with One mightier and wiser than they. It is an earnest labor of entreaty and supplication. This was the kind of prayer Hannah engaged in when she begged God for a son (1:12). Hezekiah prayed like this for an extension of his life (Is. 38:2, 3). Jonah pled for deliverance from the belly of the fish (Jon. 2:1). This is the term for prayer in 2 Chronicles 7:14, and Samuel was leading Israel in that sort of humility and national repentance.[7]

Mizpah, where Israel gathered, was on the main north-south road through the hill country and so accessible to all the tribes. The Philistines decided to show up as well and surprise the assembled Israelites. How did the repentant Israelites respond to the attacking Philistines? (1 Sam. 7:7, 8)

What role did each of the following play in the defeat of the Philistines? (1 Sam. 7:9–11)

• Samuel

• The Lord

• The Israelite army

Contrast the Ebenezer (stone monument to divine help) near Mizpah (1 Sam. 7:12) with the one near Aphek (4:1).

What did Israel gain from their repentance and spiritual revival?

• Politically (1 Sam. 7:13, 14)

• Spiritually (1 Sam. 7:15–17)

 FAITH ALIVE

How has God shown you in the past that you needed spiritual renewal?

How has He overcome any resistance or reluctance you may have shown to your need for renewal?

What have been the greatest blessings you have experienced because the Lord has renewed you spiritually after times of drifting away some?

1. *Spirit-Filled Life® Bible* (Nashville: Thomas Nelson Publishers, 1991), 405, map of "The Ministry of Samuel."

2. Ibid., 662, "Word Wealth: Ezra 3:11, great shout."

3. Ibid., 1041, "Word Wealth: Is. 60:1, glory."

4. Ronald F. Youngblood, "1, 2 Samuel," *The Expositor's Bible Commentary*, Vol. 3 (Grand Rapids, MI: Zondervan Publishing House, 1992), 602. Joyce G. Baldwin, *1 and 2 Samuel: An Introduction and Commentary* (Leicester, England: Inter-Varsity Press, 1988), 74.

5. "1, 2 Samuel," *The Expositor's Bible Commentary*, Vol. 3, 604.

6. Ibid., 606.

7. *Spirit-Filled Life® Bible*, 747, "Word Wealth: Job 42:10, prayed."

Lesson 3 / A Clear Voice In Confused Times
1 Samuel 8—12;
1 Chronicles 8:1–40;
9:35–44

When George V died in 1936, England looked forward to the reign of Edward VIII. George had been austere and formal, a king from the old mold. Edward was debonair, modern, a man of the world. As Prince of Wales, he had traveled around the empire making speeches and public appearances. There could be no doubt: With his movie-star good looks, athletic prowess, and social graces, Edward was exactly the kind of king the British public wanted.

Edward had a younger brother who had wilted under the authoritarian hand of their father. He stuttered badly and gladly had retired from public view to be Duke of York. When the old king died, England looked forward to a new era under the leadership of a new kind of ruler. Some of the British cabinet was not so sure about Edward. He seemed reluctant about the throne. Some of his ideas were odd. They wondered if he had the right stuff. But he was the best king at the moment. His brother would never do.

A TIME FOR A CHANGE

First Samuel 8 introduces a problem of goals and motivations. God had long anticipated establishing a monarchy in Israel (Gen. 49:8–10; Deut. 17:14–20; Judg. 17:6; 21:25). The elders of Israel were sensitive to a real dilemma when they asked for a king. Samuel, however, wondered if they were trying to get out from under God's authority.

What was the immediate problem and the solution the elders of Israel proposed? (1 Sam. 8:1–5)

How was this situation similar to the difficulty Eli had faced? (see 1 Sam. 2:12–17, 22–25)

From Samuel's interchange with the Lord, what can you infer about each of these? (1 Sam. 8:6–9)

• Why Samuel was displeased

• How God wanted Samuel to start preparing Israel for monarchy

What warnings did the Lord want Samuel to give Israel about the cold, hard realities of living in an absolute monarchy? (1 Sam. 8:10–18)

What three reasons did Israel give for wanting a king? (1 Sam. 8:19, 20)

1.

2.

3.

Even though Israel was drawing away from the Lord's direct rule by asking for a king, they never dreamed of setting up one on their own. They came to Samuel, the God-appointed priest, prophet, and judge and said, "Make us a king to judge us" (1 Sam. 8:5). What was there about Samuel's relationship to the Lord that gave him this authority in Israel's eyes (1 Sam. 8:21, 22)

FAITH ALIVE

At what points in your life would you have liked someone to tell you what to do so you wouldn't have had to wait for God to reveal His will?

What are some examples of selfish prayers that would get us into trouble if God answered them and gave us what we wanted?

EVERY INCH A KING

The Lord provided Israel with a king who was already out-wardly impressive and gifted him with the spiritual resources to be inwardly impressive as well. The human king who would rule visibly in the place of the divine King was chosen entirely by the Lord. The people of Israel were totally unaware of the Lord's choice until long after it was made.

What initial information about the man who would be Israel's first king are we given concerning these subjects?

• His family (1 Sam. 9:1, 2a)

- His appearance (1 Sam. 9:2b)

- His occupation (1 Sam. 9:3a)

- His approach to responsibilities (1 Sam. 9:3b, 4)

- His concern for others (1 Sam. 9:5)

BEHIND THE SCENES

Read the genealogies of Saul's family in 1 Chronicles 8:1–40 and 9:35–44. First Chronicles 8 records the family tree of the tribe of Benjamin from the days of the patriarch until the captivity of Jerusalem by Babylon in 586 B.C. This genealogy begins centuries before the time of King Saul and extends centuries after his day. Verses 29–40 focus on the clan from which Kish and his son Saul came. First Chronicles 9:35–44 repeats the genealogy of this clan. The genealogies of 1 Chronicles were compiled to help those who returned from the Babylonian captivity recover their place in society and their property. Remnants of Saul's family may have been among that band of pilgrims.

What means did the Lord use to steer Saul to a private meeting with Samuel? (1 Sam. 9:3–12)

WORD WEALTH

The word **seer** (1 Sam. 9:9) indicates a prophet who receives divine revelation through visions. The Hebrew term *ro'eh* comes from the common verb *ra'ah,* which means "to see," but which also has a wide range of nuances, including "to perceive," "to appear," "to discern," "to look," and "to stare." It was only natural for Hebrew speakers to describe a prophet as a "seer," since prophets frequently received messages from God through visions. However, the word *nabi'* (herald, spokesman) is the preferred Hebrew word for prophet (see 1 Sam. 3:20).[1]

The servant of Saul connected Samuel with the nearby city (1 Sam. 9:6), so they must have been at Samuel's hometown Ramah (7:17). Why was Samuel at home in Ramah at that time? (1 Sam. 9:12–14)

What did the primary characters in this story have to say to one another in preparation for Saul's anointing as king?

- The Lord to Samuel (1 Sam. 9:15–17)

- Samuel to Saul (1 Sam. 9:19, 20)

- Saul to Samuel (1 Sam. 9:21)

How did Samuel honor Saul at each of these stages during his brief stay in Ramah?

- At the ceremony (1 Sam. 9:22–24)

- In Samuel's home (1 Sam. 9:25, 26)

- As Saul was leaving (1 Sam. 9:27—10:1)

BEHIND THE SCENES

When Israelites offered a peace offering in celebration of the Lord's goodness to them, the right thigh was given to the priest and his family (Lev. 7:32, 33). This seems to have been the portion set aside for Samuel (1 Sam. 9:23, 24). But Samuel gave the special portion to his young guest Saul, who as yet did not know what the Lord had in mind for him.

What were the three signs Samuel gave Saul as evidence that it was the Lord's doing to anoint him Israel's first king?

1. (1 Sam. 10:2)

2. (1 Sam. 10:3, 4)

3. (1 Sam. 10:5, 6)

What was Saul to do after the three signs came to pass? (1 Sam. 10:7, 8)

Only the fulfillment of the third sign is described in 1 Samuel. How did this qualify Saul to be Israel's king? (1 Sam. 10:9, 10)

BEHIND THE SCENES

Samuel was the first prophet around whom a colony of young men gathered for the purpose of learning to dedicate themselves to the service of God. Such a group of prophets formed in Ramah, Samuel's hometown. Music was a significant part of their expressions of praise and was often written under the spirit of prophecy, which came upon them from the Lord.[2]

"Who is their father?" (1 Sam. 10:12). Does one become a prophet through lineage or through the power of God's Spirit? Saul's father, Kish, was not a prophet; therefore, the prophetic gift was given by God. The proverb came to be applied to anyone who appeared in any sphere of life that was radically different than his usual one.[3]

How did Saul behave after receiving a new heart and prophesying with the group of prophets? (1 Sam. 10:13–16)

FAITH ALIVE

What do you believe God wants you to do with your life in His service?

What indications has He given you that have led you to this conclusion?

ISRAEL ACCLAIMS SAUL KING

Once Saul had been notified that the Lord had chosen him to be Israel's first king, it was necessary to make the Lord's choice known among the people of God. Perhaps even more important from a practical viewpoint, it was necessary for Israel to embrace God's choice and give him their allegiance.

Samuel called a national assembly at Mizpah to present Saul as Israel's king (1 Sam. 10:17). What had been the last major event at Mizpah? (1 Sam. 7:5–12)

Describe the public confirmation of Saul's divine choice to be king according to these topics:

• God's repeated warning (1 Sam. 10:18, 19a)

• God's choice acted out (1 Sam. 10:19b, 21)

• God's special revelation through Samuel (1 Sam. 10:22)

• Saul's first impression on Israel (1 Sam. 10:23, 24)

• The written testimony (1 Sam. 10:25)

What were the various reactions within Israel to Saul's coronation? (1 Sam. 10:24, 26, 27)

What was Saul's first challenge as the new king of Israel? (1 Sam. 11:1–5)

How did Saul respond to the news of impending disaster at Jabesh Gilead? (1 Sam. 11:6–8)

How did Saul implement the rescue of Jabesh Gilead from Nahash the Ammonite king? (1 Sam. 11:9–11)

How did the reaction of each of the following to the victory at Jabesh Gilead strengthen Saul's rule over Israel?

• The people (1 Sam. 11:12)

• Saul (1 Sam. 11:13)

• Samuel (1 Sam. 11:14, 15)

 FAITH ALIVE

Beyond the formal process of selection, how do you know that God has placed someone in authority in your church?

What happens in a church when there is disagreement about whether a leader is God's choice? What happens when that disagreement is replaced by a sense of unity?

A PROPHETIC WORD ABOUT KINGS

At Ramah, Samuel privately anointed Saul king. At Mizpah, Saul's selection by God became public knowledge hailed by most but opposed by a few. At Gilgal, Israel embraced Saul's reign wholeheartedly because he had proven himself a king by delivering Jabesh Gilead. At Gilgal, Samuel passed the baton of rule to Saul by making his public farewell as judge of Israel.

What was the universal opinion of the integrity of Samuel's term of leadership over Israel? (1 Sam. 12:2–5)

What did Samuel point out had happened historically when Israel cried out to the Lord?

- In Egypt (1 Sam. 12:8)

- During the period of the judges (1 Sam. 12:9–11)

But what had Israel done differently from the past when Nahash the Ammonite threatened? (1 Sam. 12:12)

What roles did Israel and the Lord each play in putting Saul on the throne? (1 Sam. 12:1, 13)

 BEHIND THE SCENES

Throughout the first twelve chapters of 1 Samuel there is a running wordplay in the Hebrew text that is invisible in English. The names *Samuel* and *Saul* and the verb "to ask" share the same consonants, and only the consonants appear in written Hebrew. Hannah "asked" for a son and called him Samuel (1 Sam. 1:20). Israel "asked" for a king and got Saul (12:13, where the "ask" verb is translated "desired"). The Hebrew verb *sha'al* appears five times in the birth narrative of Samuel and six times in the coronation account of Saul. Both men appeared as a result of intense asking.

What were the spiritual choices and their consequences that Samuel set before Israel and Saul at the Gilgal coronation? (1 Sam. 12:14, 15)

Wheat was harvested in May or June well after the winter rainy season. What was the crop-threatening thunderstorm supposed to communicate to Israel and Saul? (1 Sam. 12:16–18)

Why do you think Israel asked Samuel to pray for them? (1 Sam. 12:19)

What obligations did Samuel place on each of these?
* Israel (1 Sam. 12:20, 21)

* The Lord (1 Sam. 12:22)

* Himself (1 Sam. 12:23)

What was needed for a successful monarchy under God in Israel? (1 Sam. 12:24)

What would lead to a failed monarchy in Israel? (1 Sam. 12:25)

 FAITH ALIVE

What kind of leadership does your church need most severely right now? How could you and others seek the Lord earnestly for those leaders?

How do you think the leadership and congregation of your church can best pursue spiritual success and God's blessing?

1. *Spirit-Filled Life® Bible* (Nashville: Thomas Nelson Publishers, 1991), 407, "Word Wealth: 1 Sam. 9:9, seer."
2. Ibid., 409, note on 1 Sam. 10:5.
3. Ibid., note on 1 Sam. 10:12.

Saul:
Listening to the
World, the Flesh, and
the Devil
1 Samuel 13—31

Saul received the Holy Spirit and a new heart from the Lord (1 Sam. 10:9, 10). The Spirit led him to show courage and decisiveness in rescuing the besieged citizens of Jabesh Gilead (11:6–11). But Saul turned out like a cake that hadn't been in the oven long enough. The right ingredients were there. He looked good. The first taste was good. But he really wasn't ready clear through. Israel had rushed God to give them a king before He planned to. They got the best that was available, but there was a young guy in Bethlehem whom God had in the oven of shepherding. If Israel had waited until God's timer had gone off. . . . But then again, Saul was a good part of the heat that made a king of David.

Lesson 4/Trying to Make Things Happen Without God
1 Samuel 13—15

John Wesley made a promising start in the Church of England. He spent two and a half years assisting his father in the pastorate at Epworth, England. He was ordained a priest in the Anglican church and joined with his brother Charles and other dedicated clergymen and laity in a group known as the "Holy Club." Because these serious-minded friends followed a set pattern of study, prayer, and worship, they were dubbed "Methodists."

Wesley was deeply impressed by the doctrine of justification by faith, but was uncertain he had attained it. He and Charles responded to an appeal from the Society for Propagating the Gospel in Foreign Parts and sailed as missionaries to Georgia, the penal colony of the New World. Within three years first Charles and then John returned to England in defeat.

On the boat to America, Wesley had encountered Moravian Brethren whose deeply simple piety made a great impression on him. Back in London he sought out the Moravian meeting on Aldersgate Street. There for the first time, John Wesley found the assurance that his sins were forgiven through the sacrificial death of Christ. Equally as significant for Wesley's ministry, he there sensed the power of God's Spirit that would make him the most influential gospel preacher and writer of the 18th century.

What would have happened if King Saul had sought the Lord when his life faltered after a fast start, as John Wesley did?

We'll never know. The king who began so well, with the approval of God and the support of his subjects, proved rash and erratic under pressure.

An Impatient Warrior

First Samuel 13:1 is a difficult verse. If you look up several modern versions, you will find a variety of attempts to make sense of it. Footnotes abound explaining why translators chose the readings they did. Some suggest one uncertain year passed before the battle at Jabesh Gilead united all Israel behind Saul (1 Sam. 11), and then two years of acclaimed reign passed before the events of these chapters.

At A Glance[1]

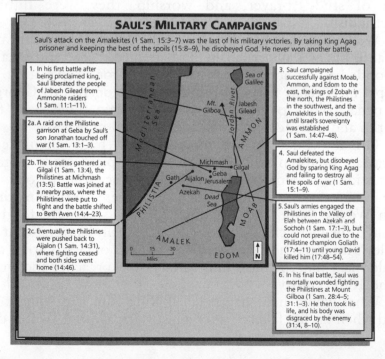

SAUL'S MILITARY CAMPAIGNS

Saul's attack on the Amalekites (1 Sam. 15:3–7) was the last of his military victories. By taking King Agag prisoner and keeping the best of the spoils (15:8–9), he disobeyed God. He never won another battle.

1. In his first battle after being proclaimed king, Saul liberated the people of Jabesh Gilead from Ammonite raiders (1 Sam. 11:1–11).

2a. A raid on the Philistine garrison at Geba by Saul's son Jonathan touched off war (1 Sam. 13:1–3).

2b. The Israelites gathered at Gilgal (1 Sam. 13:4), the Philistines at Michmash (13:5). Battle was joined at a nearby pass, where the Philistines were put to flight and the battle shifted to Beth Aven (14:4–23).

2c. Eventually the Philistines were pushed back to Aijalon (1 Sam. 14:31), where fighting ceased and both sides went home (14:46).

3. Saul campaigned successfully against Moab, Ammon, and Edom to the east, the kings of Zobah in the north, the Philistines in the southwest, and the Amalekites in the south, until Israel's sovereignty was established (1 Sam. 14:47–48).

4. Saul defeated the Amalekites, but disobeyed God by sparing King Agag and failing to destroy all the spoils of war (1 Sam. 15:1–9).

5. Saul's armies engaged the Philistines in the Valley of Elah between Azekah and Sochoh (1 Sam. 17:1–3), but could not prevail due to the Philistine champion Goliath (17:4–11) until young David killed him (17:48–54).

6. In his final battle, Saul was mortally wounded fighting the Philistines at Mount Gilboa (1 Sam. 28:4–5; 31:1–3). He then took his life, and his body was disgraced by the enemy (31:4, 8–10).

What was Israel's standing peacetime army like? (1 Sam. 13:2)

Peace was short-lived. Describe the following aspects of the new flare-up of trouble with the Philistines.
- Its cause (1 Sam. 13:3a)

- Israel's mobilization (1 Sam. 13:3b, 4)

- The Philistine threat (1 Sam. 13:5)

- Israel's morale problem (1 Sam. 13:6, 7)

Either Samuel had once again instructed King Saul to wait up to seven days for him at Gilgal (1 Sam. 10:8), or the prophet and king had a standing arrangement that they would meet at Gilgal within seven days of any national emergency.[2] Describe the following sequence that occurred at Gilgal.

- Saul's first problem (1 Sam. 13:8)

- Saul's response to his first problem (1 Sam. 13:9)

- Saul's second problem (1 Sam. 13:10)

- Saul's response to his second problem (1 Sam. 13:11, 12)

KINGDOM EXTRA

Spiritual leadership differs radically from this world's ideas about how to lead. God's leaders must realize that they represent Him in their role, since He has given them their authority. In order to honor God, His servants must be faithful both to Him and to His people.

Leaders, do not act presumptuously. Obedience will establish your authority.[3]

What did Samuel tell Saul would result from his rash disobedience? (1 Sam. 13:13, 14)

How had Israel's military preparedness deteriorated? (1 Sam. 13:2, 15)

How did the Philistines probe the weakness of the Israelite defenses? (1 Sam. 13:17, 18)

What great advantage did the Iron Age-Philistines have over the Bronze Age-Israelites? (1 Sam. 13:19–23)

FAITH ALIVE

Why do you think God makes us wait on Him sometimes when we want to make things happen?

You will notice that Saul always tried to rationalize his disobedience until he could no longer. When do you feel most tempted to justify your sin?

A Shortsighted Commander

Once a leader starts giving in to pressure, his judgment will be impaired. Saul began with simple impatience. He had a task to do and waiting for God's schedule seemed to complicate his leadership. But Saul's impatience led on to shortsightedness—acting before he thought through all the ramifications of his plans.

Describe the following aspects of the next difficulty in Saul's reign.

• The instigator (1 Sam. 14:1)

• The royal role (1 Sam. 14:2)

• Saul's spiritual adviser in place of Samuel (1 Sam. 14:3)

• The geography (1 Sam. 14:4, 5)

Describe the following aspect of Jonathan's solo action against the Philistines. (1 Sam. 14:6–14)

• The bravery involved

• Jonathan's theology of battle

• The signals to fight or withdraw

• The outcome

Describe the following aspects of Israel's follow-up on Jonathan's heroic attack on the Philistine garrison. (1 Sam. 14:15–23)

- All the resultant trembling

- King Saul's helter-skelter orders

- The Philistine chaos

- The Israelite bandwagon

In what ways is it correct to say that "the LORD saved Israel that day"? (1 Sam. 14:23)

In how many ways was King Saul's vow not to eat during the day of battle a shortsighted bit of military strategy? (1 Sam. 14:24–32)

How did Saul's shortsightedness in each of these instances keep Israel from winning an even greater victory over the Philistines?

- The slaughter of the animals (1 Sam. 14:31–35)

- The death sentence imposed on Jonathan (1 Sam. 14:36–45)

WORD WEALTH

The Hebrew word translated **roll** appears in many sacrificial settings. The place name *Gilgal* came from this term and may indicate that the stones taken from the Jordan when Israel crossed were rolled together there (Josh. 4:19, 20). Gilgal also represented God rolling the offense of Egypt off of Israel (Josh. 5:9). Galilee ("Circuit") and Golgotha ("Skull") derive from this word, as do the common nouns for wheel, whirlwind, and scroll.[4]

In 1 Samuel 14:1–46, how did Saul's prestige decline and Jonathan's increase?

First Samuel records a selection of events that reveal fatal flaws in King Saul's spiritual character. First Samuel 14:47–52 also gives a sweeping overview of his entire reign. How did Saul fare in each of these areas?

• Military campaigns to the east (Moab, Ammon, Edom), north (Zobah), west (Philistines), and south (Amalekites) (1 Sam. 14:47, 48)

• Building a family (1 Sam. 14:49–51)

• Facing his fiercest foe (1 Sam. 14:52)

FAITH ALIVE

Are you more likely to be shortsighted when you are rushed or when you are calm? Why?

When you need to think about the long-term ramifications of a decision, whom or what do you count on to help you find the mind of God?

A CARELESS SPIRITUAL LEADER

As time went along King Saul's institutional power increased but his personal authority started slipping away. He knew that the people loved his son Jonathan more than they loved him. He knew that his decisions made under pressure were being questioned. The opinion of people around him began to count more and more. What would Saul do if the will of God and the will of the people came into conflict?

What obligation did King Saul have to each of the following? (1 Sam. 15:1)

• The prophet Samuel

• The people of Israel

• The Lord

The Amalekites were descendants of Esau (Gen. 36:12, 16) who lived in extreme southern Canaan and the northern parts of the Sinai peninsula (Num. 13:29). Five centuries earlier, the Amalekites had harassed Israel during the Exodus from Egypt. God had announced their doom at that time (Ex. 17:14–16; Num. 24:20; Deut. 25:17–19). What mission did the Lord commit to King Saul through Samuel? (1 Sam. 15:2, 3)

Describe the following steps Saul took in preparation to carry out a holy war against the Amalekites.

- Assembling his forces (1 Sam. 15:4)

- Deploying his forces (1 Sam. 15:5)

- Protecting the innocent (1 Sam. 15:6)

How did Saul obey and how did he disobey the terms of God's holy war spelled out in verse 3? (1 Sam. 15:7–9)

- Obeyed

- Disobeyed

What two revelations did the Lord give Samuel about King Saul after the battle with the Amalekites?

1. (1 Sam. 15:10, 11)

2. (1 Sam. 15:12)

How did King Saul assess his obedience and the army's obedience to the command of the Lord to annihilate Amalek?

- His obedience (1 Sam. 15:13)

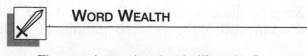

• The army's obedience (1 Sam. 15:15)

Why should remembering his spiritual history have prompted King Saul to carry out the Lord's commands diligently? (1 Sam. 15:17–19)

Why should remembering your own spiritual history affect your obedience?

How did Saul's story change as Samuel kept hammering away about the king's disobedience?

1. (1 Sam. 15:13, 15)

2. (1 Sam. 15:20, 21)

3. (1 Sam. 15:24)

Saul thought it sounded spiritual to keep the best livestock for a big offering to God. It may be that Agag was to be executed as the cream of the Amalekites along with the prize animals. What was wrong with Saul's reasoning? (1 Sam. 15:22, 23a)

WORD WEALTH

The word translated **rebellion** (1 Sam. 15:23) usually described the Israelites in the wilderness when they murmured against God. **Witchcraft** is a difficult Hebrew noun that seems to have various forms of fortune-telling in view. To rebel against

God is taking the future into your own hands to try and make life come out the way you want it rather than the way God does. It makes your stubborn will a little god (idolatry) in opposition to the Lord of hosts.

 KINGDOM EXTRA

Belief results in obedience; what we practice provides evidence of our faith. Faith is not merely a propositional affirmation. It determines action, produces obedience, and, through overcoming, becomes fruitful.

Saul illustrates that incomplete obedience reveals the same hellish attitudes as disobedience. Obey the Lord completely and do not turn away from Him.[5]

What word from God finally jolted King Saul sufficiently that he admitted his sin and begged for forgiveness? (1 Sam. 15:23b, 26)

Why do you imagine King Saul was so desperate that the prophet Samuel accompany him to the public worship that marked the victory over Amalek? (1 Sam. 15:25, 30)

Describe the following steps in divine judgment on King Saul.

1. Judgment on Saul's dynasty (1 Sam. 13:13, 14a)

2. Judgment on Saul's own reign (1 Sam. 15:27, 28a)

3. Replacement of Saul (1 Sam. 13:14b; 15:28b)

Why was it right for Samuel to execute the Lord's sentence of death on Agag? Why would it have been wrong for Saul to do it? (1 Sam. 15:32, 33)

Samuel's home at Ramah and Saul's home at Gibeah were within ten miles of each other. What was the prophet of God's relationship with the rejected king from this time? What did it picture of God's attitude? (1 Sam. 15:34, 35)

FAITH ALIVE

When Jesus described the lukewarm obedience of the Laodicean church (Rev. 3:14–22)—an obedience similar to Saul's—He said it made Him want to vomit. In what areas of life do you need to beware of halfhearted obedience that will displease the Lord?

King Saul compromised his obedience to win the favor of his soldiers who wanted to take the best of what was God's. In what kinds of situations is peer pressure an enemy to your complete obedience to the Lord?

1. *The Word in Life Study Bible* (Nashville: Thomas Nelson Publishers, 1996), 514, map of "Saul's Military Campaigns."

2. Joyce G. Baldwin, *1 and 2 Samuel: An Introduction and Commentary* (Leicester, England: Inter-Varsity Press, 1988), 104.

3. *Spirit-Filled Life® Bible* (Nashville: Thomas Nelson Publishers, 1991), 439, "Truth-in-Action through 1 Samuel."

4. Ibid., 904, "Word Wealth, Prov. 16:3, commit."

5. Ibid., 438, "Truth-in-Action through 1 Samuel."

Lesson 5/Feeling It All Slip Away
1 Samuel 16—20;
1 Chronicles 2:3–17

One day, Tom Sawyer faced a new boy in town on a visit. "A new-comer of any age or either sex was an impressive curiosity in the poor little shabby village of St. Petersburg. This boy was well dressed, too—well dressed on a week-day. . . . He had shoes on—and it was only Friday. He even wore a necktie, a bright bit of ribbon. . . . The more Tom stared at the splendid marvel, the higher he turned up his nose at his finery and the shabbier and shabbier his own outfit seemed to him to grow. Neither boy spoke. If one moved, the other moved—but only sidewise, in a circle; they kept face to face and eye to eye all the time. Finally Tom said:

'I can lick you!'
'I'd like to see you try it.'
'Well, I can do it.'
'No you can't, either.'
'Yes I can.'
'No you can't.'
'I can.'
'You can't.'
'Can!'
'Can't!' "[1]

After more posturing and strutting, the two boys fought because both wanted to be top dog. When Saul—the big handsome success—grew jealous of David—the cheerful, helpful newcomer—David didn't want to fight. It's hard for jealousy to escalate when the other party wishes you well, but Saul could read God's writing on the wall, and he fought with fiendish jealousy.

THE SPIRIT LEAVES SAUL FOR DAVID

Even though Saul was still king, the biblical narrative focuses more and more on David, the future king. Saul knew that God's eye was elsewhere, and his spirit was deeply troubled. But he never went to the Lord or Samuel to restore his spiritual relationship with God. He struggled ahead on his own. The results soon became disastrous.

What was Samuel's response to Saul's spiritual failure as king of Israel? (1 Sam. 15:35; 16:1a)

What was the Lord's response to Saul's spiritual failure as king of Israel? (1 Sam. 16:1b)

WORD WEALTH

Mourn translates the Hebrew verb *'abal*. *'Abal* means to weep, to droop, to sink down, or to lament. This term occurs more than forty times in the Old Testament and refers to mourning over a death, over sin, or over the tragedies surrounding the captivity of Jerusalem (Is. 66:10). In 1 Samuel 16:1 *'abal* describes the reaction of a prophet in whom the Spirit of God dwelt to a spiritual child gone astray from the Lord in rebellion against the anointing of that same Holy Spirit.[2]

What was the problem Samuel foresaw about anointing David king and the solution God suggested? (1 Sam. 16:2, 3)

Why do you think the elders of Bethlehem may have feared Samuel's presence among them? (1 Sam. 16:4, 5)

Why do you think the Lord made Samuel examine each of Jesse's older sons before He revealed to the prophet that David was His chosen one? (1 Sam. 16:6–12)

 BIBLE EXTRA

Read 1 Chronicles 2:3–17 where the genealogy of David's family is traced from Jacob's son Judah through the sons of David's sisters who became important military figures during David's reign. Judah was not the first-born son of Jacob, but his genealogy is placed ahead of his older brothers born to Leah because King David came from this tribe. First Samuel 16:10, 11 indicates David was Jesse's eighth son, but 1 Chronicles 2:15 says he was the seventh. It may be that one of David's older brothers had no children and was not counted in the Chronicler's family tree.[3]

 KINGDOM EXTRA

To gain wisdom means to learn to think God's thoughts after Him, esteeming the things He esteems and despising the things He despises. Among the lessons of divine wisdom: 1) Do not overvalue size. The Lord accomplished great things through small means. 2) Know that the Lord looks on the heart, not the outward appearance. Do not judge based upon what you see. 3) Do not despise small opportunities. They prepare us for bigger battles.[4]

After Samuel went home to Ramah after anointing David to be the next king of Israel, his ministry was essentially over as far as the pages of the Bible are concerned. Why do you think Samuel's ministry effectively ended with coming of the Holy Spirit on David? (1 Sam. 16:13)

 KINGDOM EXTRA

The anointing by Samuel was the first of three anointings David experienced. The second was as king over Judah (see 2 Sam. 2:4), and the third was as king over all Israel (see 5:3). At his first anointing the Spirit came upon David to equip him and direct him in the details of his life and rulership. In like manner, the Spirit who abides in us anoints us today, teaching, equipping, and directing us in the details of our lives and ministries.[5]

What spiritual problem beset Saul as soon as David was anointed, and how did Saul's advisers propose dealing with it? (1 Sam. 16:14–18)

 BEHIND THE SCENES

The **distressing spirit from the LORD** illustrates that in the absence of the Spirit of God, men are vulnerable to evil spirits. God is sovereign in all realms, physical and spiritual. However, unless we submit to Him and His rule, we are no longer protected from evil and its destructive effects. It is in this sense that God is said to have sent the Spirit. Saul was not just suffering from a depressed mental state with periods of extreme anxiety; he was being driven by an evil spirit.[6]

How did Saul's recruitment of David illustrate Samuel's predictions about monarchy? (1 Sam. 16:19, 20; see 8:10–17)

What was David's impact upon Saul in their initial encounters? (1 Sam. 16:21–23)

KINGDOM EXTRA

The profound impact of music as an instrument of spiritual warfare is demonstrated in this passage (1 Sam. 16:22, 23). David made this declaration for his own life in Psalm 32. Incorporating worship in song as a part of warfare will both drive back the enemy and invigorate the believer's soul.[7]

FAITH ALIVE

The New Testament warns believers in Jesus Christ not to grieve or quench the Holy Spirit (Eph. 4:30; 1 Thess. 5:19). How do you think we grieve and quench the Spirit in our lives?

What do you think are the dangers we face in our spiritual lives if we refuse to yield to the Spirit's control and filling of our daily lives and ministry?

COURAGE LEAVES SAUL FOR DAVID

Without the Spirit of God to direct the details of his life and reign, King Saul found it difficult to chart a long-term course of state. He could only react to the moment. But without confidence from God's leadership, he found it impossible to lead courageously.

How did the stalemate between the armies of Israel and the Philistines come about? (1 Sam. 17:1–3, 20b, 21)

Describe Goliath, the champion of the Philistine army. (1 Sam. 17:4–7)

What was the effect of the daily confrontations between Goliath and the Israelite army? (1 Sam. 17:8–11)

What was the relationship of Jesse's family to the Israelite army and the stalemate with the Philistines? (1 Sam. 17:12–16)

How did David, a civilian, end up accepting Goliath's challenge to single combat? (1 Sam. 17:17–32)

How did David reason that a young shepherd could defeat the Philistine giant Goliath? (1 Sam. 17:34–39)

Contrast David and Goliath physically and spiritually. (1 Sam. 17:40–47)

 KINGDOM EXTRA

With great faith in our Lord we can meet any challenge with courage, even in the face of insurmountable odds. David was skilled in the use of the sling but his trust was in the Lord, who had shown David His delivering power during past crises (1 Sam. 17:34–37). The "good fight of faith" (1 Tim. 6:12) entails a bold yet balanced approach to life's challenges: As human abilities are made available to the Lord, He empowers those who completely trust Him and works great exploits for His kingdom.[8]

How did David defeat Goliath? (1 Sam. 17:48–51)

How did each of these follow up on David's defeat of Goliath? (1 Sam. 17:52–58)

• The army of Israel and Judah

• David

• King Saul

It seems strange that Saul acted as though he did not recognize David (1 Sam. 17:55). It may be that Saul had never imagined David a warrior whose family background he needed to know. David also could have been one of several court musicians, and when the evil spirit left him alone Saul may have ignored David.

How do you imagine King Saul may have felt after a shepherd boy showed the God-given courage it took to fight Goliath?

 FAITH ALIVE

When have you backed away from a challenge in your life because you lacked the spiritual courage to face it in the power of God's Spirit?

What challenge are you facing right now for which you need to draw courage from the power of God's Spirit?

Popularity Leaves Saul for David

It's sad but true that Saul was troubled more by the loss of popularity than he was by the loss of God's Spirit and his courage. He could fake courage and keep up external religious appearances, but he either had or didn't have popular approval.

Who does 1 Samuel 18 report grew to love David?

1. (v. 1; see 14:1) _____

2. (v. 20) _____

3. (v. 16) _____

How did David's popularity grow to be greater than King Saul's? (1 Sam. 18:4–7)

What was King Saul's reaction to David's growing popularity within his family and among the general populace of Israel? (1 Sam. 18:8, 9)

What happened to Saul when he gave in to his anger and became suspicious of David? (1 Sam. 18:10, 11)

What deeper spiritual problem lay behind King Saul's jealousy? (1 Sam. 18:12–15)

Why was Saul considering the marriage of his first-born daughter and David, his secretly dreaded foe? (1 Sam. 18:17–19)

Why did David hesitate so long that Merab married another? (1 Sam. 18:18, 19)

How did Saul try to use his daughter's love for David as a way of destroying David? (1 Sam. 18:20–25)

What was the outcome of King Saul's cunning schemes to remove David by putting him in lethal situations against the Philistines? (1 Sam. 18:26–30)

FAITH ALIVE

What is the difference between popularity based on worldly success or fame and popularity based on character and spiritual power?

How can we be sure that we are admiring Christian leaders and friends for godly reasons rather than worldly ones?

LOYALTY LEAVES SAUL FOR DAVID

Popularity can be a fickle thing. King Saul could have waited out a momentary public frenzy about David if it had been a fad. But David's popularity tended to turn into intense loyalty. Saul had inspired that kind of loyalty only in the residents of Jabesh Gilead whom he had rescued at the very start of his reign (1 Sam. 31:11–13). David did it everywhere without trying.

How did Jonathan react when he first learned that his father wanted to kill David and remove him as a rival for the throne? (1 Sam. 19:1–7)

What prompted King Saul to go back on the promise he made to Jonathan to quit trying to kill David? (1 Sam. 19:8, 9)

How intent on killing David had Saul become at this point through the influence of the evil spirit? (1 Sam. 19:10, 11)

When Michal, King Saul's daughter, learned that her father wanted to kill her husband David, how did she react? (1 Sam. 19:12–17)

What happened to Saul's messengers and then to Saul himself when they tried to apprehend David while he conferred with the prophet Samuel? (1 Sam. 19:18–24)

Why do you think the Lord chose to express the protective presence of the Holy Spirit around Samuel and David by the same means by which He initially confirmed His choice of Saul as king? (see 1 Sam. 10:10–13)

Perhaps at Samuel's instruction, David met with Jonathan to try to determine whether King Saul had broken permanently with him (David). How did David and Jonathan differ in their initial assessment of the situation? (1 Sam. 20:1–3)

How did David propose testing the seriousness of King Saul's hostility toward him? (1 Sam. 20:4–7)

David and Jonathan pack their solemn conversation with serious pledges and requests. What momentous issues did they discuss? (1 Sam. 20:8–17)

BIBLE EXTRA

David honored his covenant with Jonathan all his life. He would not injure Jonathan's father, King Saul, because he was the Lord's anointed king (1 Sam. 24:6; 26:11). David dreaded the prospect of accompanying the Philistine army against Saul and Jonathan. The Lord spared him any involvement at the battle in which both men died (29:4). David took vengeance on those who tried to curry favor with him by harming the family of Jonathan (2 Sam. 1:14–16; 4:8–12. Eventually David brought Jonathan's maimed son, Mephibosheth, to live with him in the palace (9:1–13).

What was the signal Jonathan devised to let David know whether it was safe for him to return to Saul's court or whether he must flee in exile? (1 Sam. 20:18–23)

How did King Saul react to David and to Jonathan when David was absent from the royal feast? (1 Sam. 20:24–34)

WORD WEALTH

The Hebrew term for **anger** is a common and colorful word. Anger is mentioned approximately 250 times in the Old Testament. The word literally means "nose" or "nostrils" and calls attention to the way fierce or agitated breathing shows the presence of violent anger. King Saul's wrath was obvious as his nostrils flared and he snorted with rage.[9]

What do you think were the emotional states of Jonathan and David as the scene with the signal arrows unfolded? (1 Sam. 20:35–40)

What places do both sorrow and peace have in this farewell encounter between David and Jonathan? (1 Sam. 20:41, 42)

FAITH ALIVE

Who are the friends to whom you are bound by ties of Christian love and commitment?

How could you strengthen your faithfulness and commitment as a Christian friend?

1. Samuel L. Clemens, *The Adventures of Tom Sawyer* (New York: Dodd, Mead & Company, 1958), 7, 8.
2. *Spirit-Filled Life® Bible* (Nashville: Thomas Nelson Publishers, 1991), 1278, "Word Wealth, Joel 1:9, mourn."
3. Ronald F. Youngblood, "1, 2 Samuel," *The Expositor's Bible Commentary*, Vol. 3 (Grand Rapids, MI: Zondervan Publishing House, 1992), 684.
4. *Spirit-Filled Life® Bible*, 439, "Truth-in-Action through 1 Samuel."
5. *Hayford's Bible Handbook* (Nashville: Thomas Nelson Publishers, 1995), 71, "Surveying 1 Samuel," note on 1 Sam. 16:13.
6. *Spirit-Filled Life® Bible*, 418, note on 1 Sam. 16:14.
7. *Hayford's Bible Handbook*, 71, "Surveying 1 Samuel," note on 1 Sam. 16:22, 23.
8. Ibid., note on 1 Sam. 17:38–51.
9. *Spirit-Filled Life® Bible*, 365, "Word Wealth, Judg. 10:7, anger."

Lesson 6/Alone at the Top
1 Samuel 21—26

Shakespeare's *Hamlet* is a great play, not because scholars say it is and famous actors have played in it for centuries. *Hamlet* is a great play because Hamlet is a complex character who makes us think about how we live our own lives.

Some people think Hamlet meditated so much on all sides of issues he couldn't make up his mind. He spent days pondering the obvious treachery of his uncle against his father. He uttered the famous "To be or not to be" soliloquy in this vein.

Others think Hamlet was depressed. These contend that the Danish prince wasn't all that rational. His vacillation indicated that his emotions and personality were falling apart.

Still others think that Shakespeare created a character obsessed with vengeance whose best thoughts and noblest feelings could not keep him from rash, destructive behavior. The ghost of his father obsessed Hamlet and drove him to revenge.

That's fiction; but in real life an evil spirit drove Saul, the first king of Israel, to pursue David. In his rational moments Saul saw the truth and hated what he did. When the evil spirit was on him, the king ignored everything else in his attempts to annihilate David.

GOOD-BYE PASTORAL GUIDANCE

Saul's evil spirit had convinced him that many officials in the kingdom were plotting with David against him. When no one else saw things that way, Saul interpreted that as evidence of how deep the plot against him and for David was. Not surprisingly, King Saul began to purge from the kingdom those he suspected of aiding and abetting David in his escape.

When he showed up at the tabernacle alone and in obvious haste, how did David satisfy Ahimelech's concerns? (1 Sam. 21:1, 2)

What did David want from the priest, and what did Ahimelech give him? (1 Sam. 21:3–10)

 BEHIND THE SCENES

When the **showbread** was replaced it could be eaten but usually only by the priests. The showbread was twelve loaves made of pure wheat flour that were set in the sanctuary before Yahweh, fresh every Sabbath day. Jesus referred to this event in teaching that He was Lord of the Sabbath and that human need must be considered before ritual (Matt. 12:3, 4).[1]

What premonition do you get from knowing that an official of Saul—an Edomite no less—was there when David talked Ahimelech into helping him? (1 Sam. 21:7)

AT A GLANCE

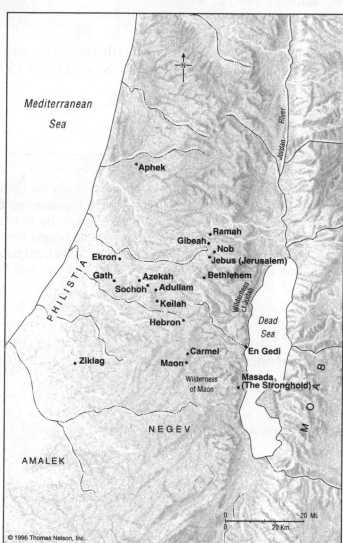

Before David Became King. Near Sochoh David defeated the giant Goliath (1 Sam. 17). Once Saul's wrath was kindled against the shepherd soldier, David fled Saul's presence and journeyed to Adullam. Taking his family to the safety of Moab, he established camp at the stronghold (1 Sam. 22:4), now known as Masada. From there his activity took him north to Aphek and south to Amalek.[2]

What was David's problem with finding refuge in the Philistine city of Gath, especially while carrying Goliath's sword? (1 Sam. 21:10–12, see 17:4)

How did David get away from Gath once the city rulers had decided he was a threat to them? (1 Sam. 21:13–15)

 BIBLE EXTRA

David wrote Psalms 34 and 56 in reflection on the Lord's deliverance from the terrors and tight places represented by Gath and King Achish. Psalm 56 is David's prayer for deliverance from his great trouble ("My enemies would hound me all day" [v. 2]). Psalm 34 is his song of jubilation that the Lord delivered him and his appeal that we also "taste and see that the LORD is good" (v. 8).

Once David found he could not hide from King Saul among the Philistines, what did he accomplish in each of these places?

1. The cave of Adullam (1 Sam. 22:1, 2)

2. Mizpah in Moab (1 Sam. 22:3, 4)

3. The stronghold (1 Sam. 22:5)

BEHIND THE SCENES

The prophet Gad probably came to David from Samuel's school of the prophets. He may also have identified with David's cause and remained with David to assist him. Through his long and constant attendance on him, Gad became known as "David's seer" (2 Sam. 24:11).[3]

What was Saul's attitude toward the loyalty of the members of his court? (1 Sam. 22:6–8)

What was Saul's accusation against Ahimelech the priest? (1 Sam. 22:11–13)

How did Ahimelech the priest defend himself against Saul's accusations? (1 Sam. 22:14, 15)

What happened when Saul ordered the execution of the priests of the Lord? (1 Sam. 22:16, 17)

What role did Doeg the Edomite play in Saul's irrational attack on Ahimelech's loyalty? (1 Sam. 22:9, 10, 18, 19)

Saul and Doeg contributed to the ongoing tragic fulfillment of the Lord's judgment on the family of Eli (1 Sam. 2:27–33). What became of the one survivor of Doeg's massacre of the priestly family and village? (1 Sam. 22:20–23)

What was the irony of Saul's massacre of the priests of the Lord as far as the future of priestly guidance for Saul and for David, the enemy Saul was obsessed with isolating and killing?

FAITH ALIVE

How do you find consolation from the Lord when you are discouraged by loneliness?

David wrote psalms to the Lord when he was alone. Read Psalm 34, which David probably wrote in the cave of Adullam. Copy out the verse that would encourage you most in a lonely moment.

GOOD-BYE HOPE

Very quickly circumstances confirmed that the Spirit of God was guiding the steps of David, while the evil spirit was serving God's purposes and confusing the steps of King Saul. Even when it seemed that Saul must finally catch his illusive prey, the Lord sovereignly used unlikely means to guard David's path.

What did David do when he received contradictory directions from the Lord and from the band of men he led concerning defending the residents of Keilah? (1 Sam. 3:1–5)

Why did David and King Saul have such different opinions about the wisdom of entering the walled city of Keilah? (1 Sam. 23:6–8)

What were David's options and how did he decide what to do when he heard that King Saul was bringing an army against him at Keilah? (1 Sam. 23:9–13)

BEHIND THE SCENES

The priestly ephod was a garment with breastplate with a pouch holding the Urim and Thummim, which were some sort of objects through which the Lord revealed his will (Ex. 28:30). At Keilah David asked a series of yes-no questions to which the priest Abiathar found the answers, presumably through the use of the Urim and Thummim.

How did the Lord encourage David after it became clear that he would have to keep moving among various wilderness hideouts rather than settling in one place? (1 Sam. 23:14–18)

What was the dream that David and Jonathan shared as friends and spiritual brothers? (1 Sam. 23:17, 18)

How did King Saul finally corner David and prepare to pounce on him? (1 Sam. 23:19–26)

How did the Lord deliver David from Saul's sure-fire trap? (1 Sam. 23:27–29)

 BEHIND THE SCENES

The strongholds at En Gedi (Masada, Hebrew *met-zadot)* were in the area of the Dead Sea. This was the place where Jewish guerrillas took refuge during the revolts of A.D. 66 and 70. Masada is just to the south. The entire area is filled with caves that served as hiding places for David and his men.[4]

What did King Saul's obsession drive him to do as soon as he had dealt with the Philistines? (1 Sam. 24:1, 2)

What happened the second time David had an opportunity to kill Saul and rid himself of this demonically driven man? (1 Sam. 24:3–7)

BEHIND THE SCENES

To tear or cut the corner from a ruler's robe was a sign of rebellion in the ancient Near East.[5] Samuel may have alluded to this kind of symbolic act when Saul accidentally tore the prophet's robe and Samuel said the kingdom was being torn from Saul (1 Sam. 15:27, 28). David quickly regretted doing something with such rebellious overtones.

When David revealed himself to King Saul from a distance outside the cave, how many different things do you think he tried to communicate to the demonically driven king? (1 Sam. 24:8–15)

How did Saul respond to David's sparing his life in each of these areas? (1 Sam. 24:16–22)

• His emotions

• His confessions about the present

• His expectations for the future

- His desire to protect his offspring

FAITH ALIVE

What has been the most memorable incident of divine guidance in your life?

How do you distinguish the guidance of God from your own wishes and ideas?

GOOD-BYE WISDOM

As time passed the guidance of the Lord in David's life took on more of the form of restraint. The longer he fled from demon-driven King Saul, the more warfare and fighting characterized his life. But the Lord did not let David become a brutal man. He restrained him by His Spirit's use of various means.

First Samuel 25 begins and ends with notes of loss for David. What were they, and how do you imagine they made him feel? (vv. 1, 44)

What kind of people were the wealthy man and his wife whom David met at Carmel in sheep country southeast of Hebron? (1 Sam. 25:2, 3)

- Nabal (his name means "Fool")

- Abigail (her name means "My Father Is Joy")

What was the purpose of the delegation of ten young men whom David sent to Nabal? (1 Sam. 25:4–9)

How did a state of hostility develop between Nabal and David? (1 Sam. 25:7–13)

How did Abigail end up playing peacemaker between her husband and David? (1 Sam. 25:14–20)

How did Abigail's approach to David deflect the anger of his intention toward Nabal? (1 Sam. 25:21–24)

How did Abigail do each of the following in her speech to David? (1 Sam. 25:25–31)

- Protect her husband

- Admit her husband's fault

- Appeal to David's spiritual strengths

- Speak the word of the Lord to David

 BEHIND THE SCENES

This is one of several instances in Scripture where strong and capable women were used by God in crucial situations. Abigail certainly showed herself worthy to be a queen, standing in stark contrast with Nabal "the fool." [6]

Why did David bless the Lord, Abigail, and her advice as he reflected on God's restraint on his anger? (1 Sam. 25:32–35)

Why do you think the news of his narrow escape had the effect of inducing something like a stroke that served as God's means of judgment on Nabal? (1 Sam. 25:36–38)

How did Nabal's death vindicate the wise action of Abigail and the spiritual restraint of David? (1 Sam. 25:39)

Why do you think David wanted Abigail as his wife, and why do you think she wanted him as her husband? (1 Sam. 25:39b–42)

Describe the situation as King Saul came out on what proved to be his last full-scale attempt to capture David. (1 Sam. 26:1–4)

What act of audacious bravery put King Saul at David's mercy? (1 Sam. 26:5–8)

Explain David's understanding of what God had in mind for Saul. (1 Sam. 26:9, 10)

 KINGDOM EXTRA

It is a serious matter to speak against or oppose the policies of God-ordained leaders. Even when we think they are wrong, we need to be careful not to oppose God's plans for His church. Often the best course of action is to leave leaders to the judgment of God, while interceding for them. If they are promoting their own agendas rather than God's, they are in serious spiritual danger.[7]

How did David make use of having penetrated King Saul's defenses while his bodyguards slept? (1 Sam. 26:11–16)

Why do you think the Bible stresses God's intervention for David rather than David's courage? (1 Sam. 26:12b)

Why do you think Saul and David addressed each other as they did in 1 Samuel 26:17?

What does David's appeal to King Saul reveal about what he hates most about living on the run? (1 Sam. 26:18–20)

Saul said that he had "played the fool" (1 Sam. 26:21). The word translated "fool" is *nabal.* How was King Saul like Nabal, the foolish man of chapter 25?

What did David say Saul should believe about him since he had spared his life a second time? (1 Sam. 26:23, 24)

What were the last things King Saul said to David in what proved to be their last encounter? (1 Sam. 26:25)

FAITH ALIVE

How has God restrained you in the past from acting on angry impulses?

Why is it better to leave the settling of personal injustices to the Lord rather than settling them ourselves?

1. *Spirit-Filled Life®Bible* (Nashville: Thomas Nelson Publishers, 1991), 425, note on 1 Sam. 21:6.
2. Ibid., 427, map of "Before David Became King."
3. Ibid., 426, note on 1 Sam. 22:5.
4. Ibid., 429, note on 1 Sam. 23:29.
5. Ronald F. Youngblood, "1, 2 Samuel," *The Expositor's Bible Commentary*, Vol. 3 (Grand Rapids, MI: Zondervan Publishing House, 1992), 746.
6. *Spirit-Filled Life® Bible*, 431, note on 1 Sam. 25:21–31.
7. Ibid., 439, "Truth-in-Action through 1 Samuel."

Lesson 7 / The Bitter End
1 Samuel 27—31;
1 Chronicles 10

Soldiers often won't talk about the fierce battles they endured. The memories are horrid. The wounds to their souls never heal. Happy forgetfulness forms the only scabs, but hateful reminders pick them instantly away. Among the worst wounds are memories of solemn young faces waiting to go on a suicide mission.

Knowing that death could strike at any moment in the form of a bullet, bomb, or exploding mortar round is one thing. Knowing that at 0700 hours your unit will attack a machine-gun nest and suffer 90 percent casualties is another. You reckon your life is over. You tune out the voice of your will and fall back on the reflex actions of your training. Obey orders, do your job. and don't think about what's coming.

But the other soldiers who aren't going are watching you. They see your dead face and know. They may survive the war, but remembering you will be a wound that never heals.

Knowing in advance the day of your death is a terrible burden. King Saul should have never known his, but he could not wait on the Lord with confidence in His will—not even at the bitter end.

DAVID WITH THE PHILISTINES

There came a time when David could no longer run from King Saul in the Judean wilderness. Maybe he could see that the Philistine threat to Israel was approaching a new level of danger and he wanted to monitor it. Maybe he thought the Philistines easier to fool than Saul.

When David pretended to ally himself with Achish the king of Gath, what did his presence in Philistia mean to each of these people? (1 Sam. 27:1–4)

- David

- Achish

- Saul

BEHIND THE SCENES

It had been two years since David had pretended insanity in front of Achish the king of Gath to save his life (1 Sam. 21:10). He returned as an outlaw and enemy of Saul, king of Israel. Achish welcomed David—perhaps warily at first—as a potentially useful political ally. Achish may have hoped in time to lure David's tribe, Judah, away from allegiance to the rest of Israel.[1]

Achish posted David and his private army in the city of Ziklag on the border between Philistine territory and the wilderness of southern Judah (1 Sam. 27:5–7). What was David's strategy against the nomadic enemies of Judah? (1 Sam. 27:8, 9)

What did Achish think David was doing militarily and politically? (1 Sam. 27:10–12)

At the end of a year and four months as a mercenary in the service of Achish, king of Gath (1 Sam. 27:7), what dilemma did David find himself facing? (1 Sam. 28:1, 2)

SAUL WITH THE MOUNTAIN

At the very time that David was wrestling with how to maintain the appearance of loyalty to Achish without warring against King Saul and his countrymen, Saul faced a greater dilemma. He needed guidance. Saul had lost his day-to-day source of divine guidance when, in a fit of jealous rage, he ordered the massacre of the Lord's priests (1 Sam. 22:18, 19).

Two other sources of supernatural guidance were no longer available to King Saul. What were they, and why were they unavailable? (1 Sam. 28:3)

1.

2.

What were Saul's problems that had him in a panic?

• His military problem (1 Sam. 28:4, 5)

• His spiritual problem (1 Sam. 28:6)

How many things strike you as being wrong in King Saul's approach to the medium who practiced spiritism at Endor? (1 Sam. 28:7–10)

How did the medium and King Saul react to her vision of the spirit of Samuel ascending from the earth? (1 Sam. 28:11–14)

The exchange between Saul and Samuel was brutally frank on both sides. Summarize what they said to one another.

• Saul's complaints (1 Sam. 28:15)

• Samuel's prophetic messages about the past and future (1 Sam. 28:16–19)

 BEHIND THE SCENES

Before Saul and the medium could react, Samuel appeared—not a dead ghost conjured up, but a prophet of God again delivering God's message to the king. It is clear that the medium had not called him up, but that the Lord had again stepped into the life of Saul to speak to him. The woman was terrified and "cried out," literally "screamed in terror," shocked at Samuel's appearance. Far from giving credence to any kind of spiritualist activity or contacting the dead, this passage shows that God is supreme. The medium was left terrified, and Saul was paralyzed with fear, as both of them were rejected by the living God.[2]

 KINGDOM EXTRA

When King Saul failed to annihilate the Amalekites in obedience to the command of God, Samuel told him, "Rebellion is as the sin of witchcraft" (1 Sam. 15:23). There is no equivalent in the Hebrew text of this statement for the English word *as*. The connection between rebellion and witchcraft is more direct than the English translation reveals. In King Saul's case, his spiritual haste that so often led him to do things in the flesh led him directly to a literal witch at Endor.

Rebellion always is a preference for walking in the path of the world, the flesh, or the devil over living in obedience to the Word and Spirit of God. Spiritual rebellion is obedience to another "voice" and disobedience to the voice of God. Don't follow the spiritual path along which King Saul walked.

What final service did the medium of Endor provide for King Saul and his attendants? (1 Sam. 28:20–25)

How do you think King Saul must have felt sitting in the medium's dimly lit house in the middle of the night waiting for his last meal after hearing the message of doom from Samuel?

FAITH ALIVE

Satan spreads deadly snares through occult practices. People try to see the future in order to control their lives and gain success. But Satan doesn't control the future. God does. Satan is a liar and a deceiver. No matter what he promises, he delivers fear of death and discord between people (Heb. 2:14; James 3:14, 15).

How can things like horoscopes, *Ouija* boards, and seances lead to fear and discord for those who hope to gain peace and harmony from them?

How does rejoicing in the Word and Spirit of God cast out the fear and heal the divisions caused by listening to the occult messages?

DAVID DELIVERED FROM TRAGEDY

It is intriguing to wonder if David and his six hundred troops would have turned out to be a fifth column in the Philistine ranks and delivered King Saul and the Israelite army by disrupting the Philistines from within. That, however, was not in God's plan. He kept David away from the tragic end Saul faced.

The Philistine army enters and leaves the Book of 1 Samuel at the same site. What is it? (1 Sam. 4:1; 29:1)

Why did the Philistine rulers object to the presence of David and his men in their attack on Israel? (1 Sam. 29:2–5)

 WORD WEALTH

When the Philistines worried that David might become their **adversary** in battle against Israel, they used the Hebrew noun *satan*. In the Old Testament *satan* is an ordinary word for an opponent many more times than the name of the fallen angel who is the sworn adversary of the Lord God. He is *the* Satan. One who was a satan was more than a nuisance, however. A *satan* was a nemesis, a foe who always had the potential of destroying one.

How thoroughly had King Achish become convinced that David was his faithful servant? (1 Sam. 29:6–10)

Do you think David really wanted to go with Achish to the battle between the Philistines and Israel? Why or why not? (1 Sam. 29:8, 11)

What did David and his troops discover when they got home to Ziklag? (1 Sam. 30:1–3, 5)

What were the reactions of David and his men to the devastation of Ziklag and the capture of their families?

- Short-term (1 Sam. 30:4)

- Long-term (1 Sam. 30:6)

In contrast to Saul's resort to the medium of Endor, how did David find guidance for deciding what to do about the Amalekite raid on Ziklag? (1 Sam. 30:7, 8)

How did David's army, wearied from its long march home from Aphek, catch up with the Amalekites? (1 Sam. 30:9–16)

Describe the success God gave David against the Amalekites that stands in stark contrast to what was happening to King Saul at the same time many miles to the north. (1 Sam. 30:17–20)

How did David wisely use the spoils of the battle with the Amalekites to build the solidarity of his army and his solidarity with the tribe of Judah?

- Solidarity of his army (1 Sam 30:21–25)

- Solidarity with Judah (1 Sam. 30:26–31)

FAITH ALIVE

When has the clear leading of God helped you escape a difficult situation? How did God make His will known to you?

What do you think would have happened in that situation if you had felt sorry for yourself and ignored the leading of God?

SAUL DELIVERED TO TRAGEDY

The account of Saul's tragic death is remarkably restrained in the few verses of 1 Samuel 31 and its close parallel in 1 Chronicles 10. Even though he knew his destiny, King Saul fulfilled his duty as the king who would lead Israel against her enemies (1 Sam. 8:20).

What happened when the Philistine army attacked the Israelite army on the lower slopes of Mount Gilboa? (1 Sam. 31:1–3; 1 Chr. 10:1–3)

Why did Saul want his armorbearer to kill him after he was mortally wounded by Philistine archers? (1 Sam. 31:4; 1 Chr. 10:4)

How did Saul and his armorbearer die? (1 Sam. 31:4, 5; 1 Chr. 10:4, 5)

How did the Israelite army react to the death of Saul and three of his sons? (1 Sam. 31:7; 1 Chr. 10:7)

What did the Philistines do when they discovered the bodies of Saul and his sons while reconnoitering the battlefield? (1 Sam. 31:8–10; 1 Chr. 10:8–10)

How did Philistine treatment of Saul compare with David's treatment of Goliath? (see 1 Sam. 17:51, 54; 21:9)

How were the bodies of King Saul and his sons rescued from disgrace? (1 Sam. 31:11–13; 1 Chr. 10:11, 12)

BEHIND THE SCENES

Saul had saved the people of Jabesh Gilead from Nahash the Ammonite in his first military action as king (1 Sam. 11). Years later they risked their lives to express their gratitude and loyalty to Saul. The distance from Beth Shan to Jabesh Gilead is about ten or twelve miles.

David would later exhume the bones of Saul and Jonathan and take them to the family tomb at Zela in Saul's homeland of Benjamin (2 Sam. 21:12–14). Saul was crowned at about twenty years of age. He reigned forty years. Therefore he was about sixty years old at the time of his death.[3]

How did the Chronicler summarize the contributing factors that lead inexorably to the death of Saul? (1 Chr. 10:13, 14)

FAITH ALIVE

Saul did not die because he foolishly disobeyed the Lord once or twice. He built up a forty-year pattern of going his own way that left him isolated from God and doomed to destruction.

What patterns of spiritual indifference or disobedience do you need to resist in your life so that your heart does not become cold toward the Lord?

How does the Spirit of God prod and convict you to warn you against the kind of spiritual backsliding that destroyed King Saul?

1. *Spirit-Filled Life® Bible* (Nashville: Thomas Nelson Publishers, 1991), 433, note on 1 Sam. 27:1.

2. Ibid., 435, note on 1 Sam. 28:11–19.

3. Ibid., 438, notes on 1 Sam. 31:11–13.

David:
Pursuing the Heart
of God
2 Samuel 1—24;
1 Chronicles 11—29

David wrote exquisite poetry and performed music masterfully. He excelled first as a warrior and later as a military tactician. He led people sensitively, tactfully, and firmly. He praised God exuberantly and publicly. David also flaunted the commandments of God about adultery and murder as though they didn't apply to him. He repented with a broken, bleeding heart as soon as he felt the conviction of God's Spirit. He enjoyed the forgiveness of God, but suffered the consequences of his spiritual failures the rest of his life.

Lesson 8/Who's the Boss?
2 Samuel 1—4

Remember the story about Edward VIII at the beginning of Lesson 3? Edward abdicated the British throne less than a year after becoming king to marry Mrs. Wallis Simpson. As titular head of the Church of England, the British monarch can marry neither a Catholic nor a divorced person. Mrs. Simpson was both. All through 1936 the royal family stalled Edward's coronation while they made it clear he could not marry Mrs. Simpson. Edward abdicated. The world swooned over the handsome duke and the striking divorcée.

Edward's younger brother George was dragged from his happy seclusion as Duke of York and crowned George VI in the ceremony planned for Edward. George's stammer made every public appearance an ordeal, so people initially thought him cold and aloof. Edward had been so suave and personable.

But when World War II broke out, George made himself a visible monarch in every corner of London during the blitz. His teenaged daughter Elizabeth wore slacks and drove a truck in the war effort. Meanwhile, both Edward and Mrs. Simpson proved to have troublesome connections to European Nazis. The British Foreign Office stuck Edward in the Bahamas as wartime governor where he could cause no mischief.

Saul too had seemed such an obviously regal fellow. The very idea that God would prefer some poet who was content to keep sheep in Bethlehem! But that's the point. Popular opinion didn't choose George VI of Great Britain or David of Israel. But they both were the true kings.

HONORING THE LORD'S ANOINTED

Once King Saul died, you might have expected David to

pop on a crown and dance on Saul's grave. But even as he had waited for God to remove Saul, David waited for God to install him on Israel's throne. And he did not gloat over Saul's demise. David had loved Saul, both for himself and because he was Jonathan's father. He honored Saul because God had made him king—even after Saul had forfeited God's blessing and Spirit.

Describe the survivor of Israel's rout by the Philistines who made his way to David at Ziklag with news of the battle. (2 Sam. 1:2, 5, 8)

What information did David ask of the messenger? (2 Sam. 1:3–5)

What story did the young Amalekite tell David, and how did it differ from what actually happened? (2 Sam. 1:6–19; see 1 Sam. 31:3–5)

What supporting evidence had the Amalekite taken from the battle scene before the Philistines desecrated the bodies? (2 Sam. 1:10)

Why do you suppose the young Amalekite made up the story for David about killing King Saul?

How did David, his army of six hundred, and their family members react to the news of the death of Saul, three of his sons, and many in Israel's army? (2 Sam. 1:11, 12)

How did David then respond to the Amalekite messenger, and how did he justify his response? (2 Sam. 1:13–16)

WORD WEALTH

The Hebrew word translated **blood** appears 360 times in the Old Testament, starting with the introduction of sacrifice (Gen. 4:4), continuing through the Law of Moses with the offering of the blood of sacrifices (appearing in Leviticus about sixty times), and culminating in the sacrifice of God's sinless Lamb. **Blood** is the "life" of humans and animals (Lev. 17:11); therefore, sacrifice is a life for a life. Human **blood,** and the "life" it contains, must not be shed by person or beast (Gen. 9:5, 6). Animal **blood,** and the life it contains, was to be drained from meat before it was eaten (Lev. 17:12–14).[1]

According to the following topics, describe the lament David composed. (2 Sam. 1:17, 18)

- Its subject

- Its title

- Who learned it

- Where it was recorded

BEHIND THE SCENES

The Song of the Bow is an appropriate title, for not only were the bow and arrow symbols of military might but also the fighting men of Saul's tribe, Benjamin, were highly regarded for their ability with the bow and arrow. The Book of Jasher, or "The Book of the Upright," was a national songbook of Israel. It is referred to in Joshua 10:12–14 where Joshua's command, "Sun, stand still over Gibeon," is said to be recorded.[2]

The Song of the Bow is organized so the middle verses contain the main thrust of David's lament. The verses on either side of the core deal with the same topic, and so on out to the beginning and end of the song. Analyze the following portions of the Song of the Bow.

- Its core (2 Sam. 1:22, 23)

- Lament for Saul (2 Sam. 1:21, 24)

- Lament for Jonathan (2 Sam. 1:19, 25–26)

- Lament for Saul and Jonathan (2 Sam. 1:20, 27)

Even after mourning Saul and Jonathan, David did not presume to seize the throne of Israel as the anointed of the Lord. How did he determine what step to take next? (2 Sam. 2:1)

Hebron was a key city in Judah, rich in patriarchal history. Abraham (Gen. 25:9), Sarah (23:19), Isaac (35:27–29), and Jacob (50:13) were buried there by the oaks of Mamre in the burial cave Abraham bought from Ephron the Hittite (23:16). Describe how David and his entourage were welcomed by Hebron and Judah. (2 Sam. 2:2–4a)

How did David honor the residents of Jabesh Gilead for risking their lives to rescue the body of Saul? (2 Sam. 2:4b–6)

What political end may have motivated David's overture to the residents of Jabesh Gilead? (2 Sam. 2:7)

FAITH ALIVE

How can the example of David's respect for Saul, who hated him, help you in deciding how to react to those people in your life who annoy you or actively oppose you?

Why is it usually wise to move cautiously when taking the place of a leader who has been in office a long time and stirred strong reactions, both pro and con?

How do you think you should react to someone who tries to push himself or herself into prominence over existing leaders?

UNCIVIL WAR

Many people in Israel knew that David had been anointed king by Samuel years earlier. But tribal tensions led the northern tribes to resent the strength of Judah. The tribe of Benjamin felt loyalty to the family of Saul. Saul's cousin Abner, who had commanded Saul's army, saw a chance to become a kingmaker and the power behind the throne.

What was Abner's scheme? (2 Sam. 2:8, 9)

What was the political situation as the result of Abner's maneuver? (2 Sam. 2:10, 11)

BEHIND THE SCENES

Ishbosheth's actual name was Esh-baal, which means "The Man of Baal" (1 Chr. 8:33; 9:39). The writer of 1 and 2 Samuel liked to substitute the word *bosheth* ("shame") for the name of the Canaanite god Baal. Merib-Baal (1 Chr. 8:34; 9:40) becomes Mephibosheth (2 Sam. 4:4), and Jerub-Baal (Judg. 6:32) becomes Jerubbesheth (2 Sam. 11:21).

Reconciling the two-.year reign of Ishbosheth and the seven-and-one-half-year reign of David (over only the tribe of Judah) is difficult. It's hard to imagine that Abner waited five years after Saul died before promoting the claim of Ishbosheth to the throne. "The discrepancy . . . is best explained by David's refusal to seize the throne. He was content to wait [after Ishbosheth's death] until the people came to him, confirming God's anointing and timing."[3]

The capital of Israel was Mahanaim on the Jabbok River east of the Jordan. The capital of Judah was at Hebron, south of Bethlehem. The armies of the rival kingdoms met at Gibeon in the territory of Benjamin (2 Sam. 2:12, 13). How was the conflict at the pool of Gibeon decided? (2 Sam. 2:14–17)

In all likelihood Zeruiah was David's older half-sister (1 Chr. 2:16), so her sons were David's nephews, although roughly his age. Asahel was the youngest, not nearly as experienced in warfare as crafty Abner. Using the following topics, describe the one-on-one battle between Asahel and Abner. (2 Sam. 2:18–23)

- Asahel's advantage

- Abner's warning

• Asahel's death

Using the following topics, describe the battle that followed Asahel's death at Abner's hands.

• The battle positions at dusk (2 Sam. 2:24, 25)

• Abner's challenge (2 Sam. 2:26)

• Joab's response (2 Sam. 2:27, 28)

• Abner's escape (2 Sam. 2:29)

• Battle casualties (2 Sam. 2:30, 31)

• Joab's return (2 Sam. 2:32)

How did the writer of 2 Samuel summarize the course of the conflict between David and Ishbosheth? (2 Sam. 3:1)

How many wives and sons made up David's family before his seven-and-one-half-year reign in Hebron ended? (2 Sam. 3:2–5)

What series of events led to the breakdown of the relationship between King Ishbosheth and his military commander Abner? (2 Sam. 3:6–7)

How did Abner threaten his king, and how did Ishbosheth respond? (2 Sam. 3:8–11)

How did Abner act on his threat against Ishbosheth? (2 Sam. 3:12)

How did David test the genuineness of Abner's proposal to come over to his side? (2 Sam. 2:13–16)

What preliminary work did Abner do to persuade the northern tribes of Israel to support David as the king of all Israel? (2 Sam. 3:17–19)

What further plans did Abner make to convince the northern tribes to give allegiance to David? (2 Sam. 3:20, 21)

What was Joab's reaction to the news that Abner was switching his support from Ishbosheth to David? (2 Sam. 3:22–25)

What did Joab do in retaliation for his brother Asahel's death at Abner's hands? (2 Sam. 3:26, 27)

What was David's reaction to Joab's murder of Abner? (2 Sam. 3:28–30)

How did David punish Joab and distance himself from Abner's murder at the funeral for Abner? (2 Sam. 3:31–37)

What were David's comparative assessments of Abner and Joab? (2 Sam. 3:38, 39)

FAITH ALIVE

When have you seen someone badly hurt emotionally or spiritually because Christian friends quarreled and feuded over a period of time?

In what ways do you think the name of the Lord is disgraced by divisions between Christians?

How do you think the Spirit of God works to heal divisions among believers and restore peace and unity?

WARTIME JUSTICE

Abner had been the power behind the throne of Ishbosheth. Once Abner was killed by Joab, a power vacuum existed in the court of Ishbosheth in Mahanaim. Abner had started the bandwagon rolling toward declaring David king, and soon two opportunists decided to see if they could advance their careers with a spot of regicide.

Describe the main participants in the events facing the northern tribes after the death of Abner, the power behind the throne of Ishbosheth. (2 Sam. 4:1–4)

• King Ishbosheth

- The people of Israel

- The two plotting Ishbosheth's assassination

- Jonathan's son Mephibosheth

 BEHIND THE SCENES

Beeroth was a village associated with Gibeon (Josh. 9:17). Its inhabitants had been Canaanites protected by the treaty Joshua made with Gibeon. At some point the Canaanite inhabitants of Beeroth had immigrated to Gittaim near Philistine country (2 Sam. 4:3). From then on Benjamites had occupied Beeroth. Ishbosheth's assassins were his fellow tribesmen.

How did Baanah and Rechab assassinate King Ishbosheth in his royal residence in Mahanaim? (2 Sam. 4:5–7)

What do you think Baanah and Rechab set out to accomplish by assassinating King Ishbosheth? (2 Sam. 4:8)

What did David have to say about each of the following aspects of his view of the assassination of Ishbosheth?

- The precedent for his viewpoint (2 Sam. 4:9, 10)

- The moral nature of the assassination (2 Sam. 4:11a)

- The demand of justice (2 Sam. 4:11b)

WORD WEALTH

A righteous person is one who is just, clear, and clean. He or she is characterized by fairness, integrity, and justice in all his or her dealings. This Hebrew noun *tsaddiq* occurs more than two hundred times in the Old Testament. It derives from a verb that denotes living or acting justly and uprightly in relation to God and other people. It is the *tsaddiq* who shall live by his faith (Hab. 2:4). In the present verse, David attributes greater integrity and justness to the murdered Ishbosheth than to Baanah and Rechab who assassinated him.[4]

How did David demonstrate his outrage at the assassination of King Ishbosheth and show his respect for his dead opponent? (2 Sam. 4:12)

FAITH ALIVE

When someone gloats over the failures of his or her enemies, what negative things does that gloating say about the spiritual maturity of the one doing it?

When someone is gracious and concerned about the failures of his or her enemies, what positive things does that compassion say about the spiritual maturity of the one exhibiting it?

When do you think a leader in the church should wait for the Lord to put him in an authority role and when do you think he or she is justified in actively pursuing a leadership role?

1. *Spirit-Filled Life® Bible* (Nashville: Thomas Nelson Publishers, 1991), 169, "Word Wealth, Lev. 17:11, blood."
2. Ibid., 443, note on 2 Sam. 1:18.
3. Ibid., 444, note on 2 Sam. 2:10, 11.
4. Ibid., 1145, "Word Wealth, Lam. 1:18, righteous."

Lesson 9/Nothing Succeeds Like Success

2 Samuel 5—9;
1 Chronicles 11—18

A small businessman from the old country kept his accounts payable in a cigar box, his accounts receivable on a spindle, and his cash in the cash register. His college-educated son complained, "Pop, how can you run your business like this? How do you know what your profits are? Do you even have any profits?"

The old man looked at his son as though he couldn't believe his ears. "When I got off the boat, I had nothing but the pants I was wearing. Today your sister is an art teacher, your brother is a doctor, and you're an accountant. I have a house, a car, and a good business. Everything is paid for. You're the smarty. Figure it out. Add everything up and subtract the pants. That's my profit."

Nothing succeeds like success; nothing fails like failure. For King Saul spiritual failure had led to a series of poor decisions and impulsive efforts to get rid of David, who had been one of Saul's greatest assets. His kingdom ran downhill almost from the start. David began as a spiritual success, and his reign was marked by good decisions and strategic planning based on the will of God. His kingdom took off like a skyrocket.

DAVID UNITES ALL ISRAEL

Before his death Abner, Ishbosheth's general, had proposed to the elders of the northern tribes that they make David king of a reunited Israel (2 Sam. 3:17–21). Once Ishbosheth was assassinated the northern tribes took the initiative to see that David united all the tribes.

How did the elders of Israel go about arranging for David to rule over them? (2 Sam. 5:1–3; 1 Chr. 11:1–3)

Note the following statistics of David's reign. (2 Sam. 5:4, 5)

1. Age when he became king _____

2. Length of reign in Hebron _____

3. Length of reign in Jerusalem _____

4. Total reign _____

The Jebusite citadel of Salem considered itself impregnable. David knew if he conquered it, he could establish a capital city with no historic ties to any tribe. It could be a rallying point for all of Israel. Describe the capture of Jerusalem and the effects of that victory. (2 Sam. 5:6–10; 1 Chr. 11:4–9)

Describe the personal prosperity of David in his new capital Jerusalem during his reign. (2 Sam. 5:11–16; 1 Chr. 14:1–7. First Chronicles 14 has the best list of David's sons born in Jerusalem.)

BIBLE EXTRA

First Chronicles 11:10—12:40 recorded for the exiles who returned from Babylon more than five hundred years after the time of David the names of the military heroes who made David's reign great. First Chronicles 11:10–47 names the heroes who emerged from the ranks of David's army of outcasts to become known as his "mighty men." First Chronicles 12:1–22 contains the names of various groups of men and their tribal origins who had left Saul's kingdom to join with David during various stages of his flight from King Saul. They were the group from which the mighty men distinguished themselves. First Chronicles 12:23–40 lists the leaders and numbers the troops from the northern tribes who rallied to David when he became king of the northern tribes as well as Judah.

What were David's mighty men like? (1 Chr. 11:12–19, 22–25)

What kind of men had deserted Saul for David? (1 Chr. 12:1, 2, 8, 16–18)

What was the attitude of Israel's army toward making David their king? (1 Chr. 12:38–40)

As soon as all Israel made David king, the Philistines attacked him, trying to drive a wedge between the territory of Judah and Benjamin. The Valley of Rephaim penetrated the Israelite hills essentially to Jerusalem. How were the two Philistine attacks and David's responses similar and dissimilar? (2 Sam 5:1–25; 1 Chr. 14:8–17)

KINGDOM EXTRA

David and the army of Israel did not wait for a merely coincidental sign. "The wind which would cause a sound like a rushing of feet was in this case the wind of the Spirit of God. . . . David must move with the Spirit of God if he is to fulfill God's purpose to defeat the enemy. There was a place for waiting, but a place also for action."[1] Today every believer in Christ must wait for and then obey the moving of the Holy Spirit with vigor.

Jerusalem was a capital all of Israel could "own." The Philistines had been not only defeated but driven from their outposts in Israelite territory. David's final act of national unification was to bring the ark of the covenant to Jerusalem so that the City of David would also be the City of God. Describe the celebration that accompanied the movement of the ark. (2 Sam. 6:1–5; 1 Chr. 13:1–8)

What happened when David tried to move the ark of the covenant using a cart as the Philistines had done earlier? (2 Sam. 6:3–11; 1 Chr. 13:7–14)

When David moved the ark of the covenant from Obed-Edom's house to the tent he pitched for it in Jerusalem, what did the event mean to the following?

- David (2 Sam. 6:12–15, 18, 19)

- The Levites (1 Chr. 15:4–28)

- Michal (2 Sam. 6:16, 20)

- The worshiping multitude (1 Chr. 15:3, 28)

- David and Michal (2 Sam. 6:20–23)

What role did the music of praise play in the worship of the Lord before the ark of the covenant? (1 Chr. 16:4–6, 37–42)

In David's psalm of thanksgiving at the time of the ark's arrival in Jerusalem, what "wondrous works" formed the basis to "give thanks to the LORD"? (1 Chr. 16:8–22)

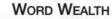

WORD WEALTH

Thank translates the Hebrew verb meaning to revere or worship with extended hands; to praise, give thanks, acknowledge, declare the merits of someone. Yadah is an important word for "praise" or "thanks" and occurs more than one hundred times in the Old Testament; more than half of these are in the Book of Psalms. The origin of this verb is the noun *yad* (hand), suggesting outstretched hands as a means of worship and thanks.[2]

In David's psalm of thanksgiving marking the ark's arrival in Jerusalem, what evidence did he give that the Lord "is great and greatly to be praised"? (1 Chr. 16:23–33)

In David's psalm of thanksgiving marking the ark's arrival in Jerusalem, what prayer did he base on the glories of God's deeds and character? (1 Chr. 16:24–36)

How did the Lord bless Obed-Edom in response to this Levite's devotion to Him? (1 Chr. 13:14; 15:18, 21; 16:38; 26:8)

KINGDOM EXTRA

David presented his psalm to the choir leader of Israel on the day the ark—signifying God's presence—was placed in the tabernacle at Jerusalem (1 Chr. 15:1; 16:1). The people were exhorted to thank the Lord for His powerful works on their behalf and His personal covenant with them—which His presence affords (vv. 8–13, 15–22).

Spirit-filled believers not only give joyful thanks for God's indwelling presence, which secures personal relationship, but they also greet in earnest the continuing fulness of His presence, whereby we experience His saving power through both our words and works.[3]

FAITH ALIVE

How can people who are troubled by joyous and expressive praise, as Michal was, open their hearts and spirits to the Spirit of God so that they can worship with all their hearts as David did?

What role can praise and worship expressed through dance, instrumental music, and vocal music play in uniting the people of God to love and serve Him?

GOD'S COVENANT WITH DAVID

The pivotal chapter in 1 and 2 Samuel—perhaps in all the historical books of the Old Testament—recounts God's covenant with David that promised him a dynasty that would last forever. Out of these promises arises the messianic hopes of Judaism that are fulfilled in Jesus Christ. The whole theology of the kingdom of God, the kingdom people, and their kingdom authority spring from God's grand promises found in 2 Samuel 7 and its restatement in 1 Chronicles 17.

What set of circumstances led to the prophetic revelation from God through Nathan concerning the future of David's dynasty? (2 Sam. 7:1–4; 1 Chr. 17:1–3)

What did the Lord think of David's proposal to build a house for Him in Jerusalem? (2 Sam. 7:5–7; 1 Chr. 17:4–6)

By what right could the Lord promise David to build him a house? (2 Sam. 7:8–11; 1 Chr. 17:7–10)

What promises did the Lord make to David concerning his "seed"? (2 Sam. 7:12–17; 1 Chr. 17:1–15)

Which of these promises do you think were fulfilled in Solomon and which had to wait for fulfillment in Jesus the Son of David?

David went into the tent that held the ark of the covenant and sat before the Lord in prayer. This may have been the position in which the king of Israel normally prayed. What did David tell the Lord about each of these subjects?

• His amazement about the present (2 Sam. 7:18–21; 1 Chr. 17:16–19)

• His gratitude about the past (2 Sam. 7:22–24; 1 Chr. 17:20–22)

• His petition for the future (2 Sam. 7:25–29; 1 Chr.

17:23–27). Notice the repetition of "forever" and "Your servant."

FAITH ALIVE

Write three of the eternal promises from God's Word that you cling to for spiritual comfort and assurance as David must have clung to the promises of the Davidic covenant.

Write some of your praises to God concerning the present, past, and future.

1. Present

2. Past

3. Future

DAVID WINS AN EMPIRE

Nearly ten centuries before the time of King David, the Lord had promised Abraham, "To your descendants I have given this land, from the river of Egypt to the great river, the River Euphrates" (Gen. 15:18). Once the Lord had entered into covenant with King David, He blessed David with a realm that covered the territory of the Abrahamic covenant.

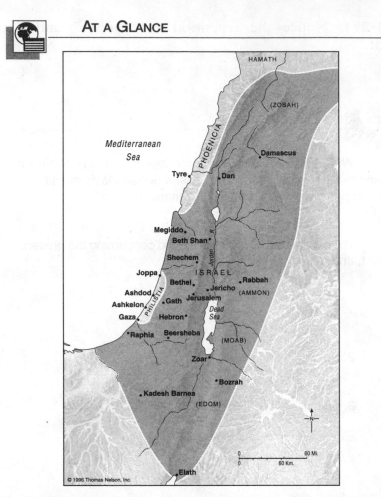

The Davidic Kingdom. David's military exploits successfully incorporated into the Israelite kingdom the powers of Edom, Moab, Ammon, and Zobah.[4]

Describe the military operations David carried out in each of these directions from Israel.

- West (2 Sam. 8:1; 1 Chr. 18:1)

- East (2 Sam. 8:2; 1 Chr. 18:2)

- North (2 Sam. 8:3–12; 1 Chr. 18:3–11)

- South (2 Sam. 8:13, 14; 1 Chr. 18:12, 13)

BEHIND THE SCENES

The Hebrew text of 1 and 2 Samuel has more difficulties in it than most books of the Old Testament. In 2 Samuel 8:1, for instance, Metheg Ammah appears where 1 Chronicles 18:1 reads Gath. In 2 Samuel 8:13 the enemy south of the Dead Sea is identified as Syrians, but 1 Chronicles 18:12 says they were Edomites. Metheg Ammah may mean "the reins of the mother (city)," in which case the expression means to take control of Gath, the leading city of the area. In Hebrew the difference between Edom and Syria (Aram) is the difference between two nearly identical consonants. At some point a scribe miscopied Edom as Aram in 2 Samuel 8:13.

What new and exotic things did David encounter in his northern campaign, and how did he react to their temptation to let them replace the Lord in his affection? (2 Sam. 8:3–12; 1 Chr. 18:3–11)

What is the repeated expression in 2 Samuel 8:6 and 14 (1 Chr. 18:6, 13)?

Why do you think the writers of 2 Samuel and 1 Chronicles credited David's victories to the Lord's preservation rather than David's prowess as a soldier?

What does 2 Samuel 8:15–18 (1 Chr. 18:14–17) tell you about the goals and organization of David's kingdom?

FAITH ALIVE

In your life how does each of these components of the kingdom of God find expression?

• The King

• The King's realm

• The King's rule over His realm

DAVID REMEMBERS JONATHAN

David, in a cedar palace in the citadel of Jerusalem at the head of an empire that reached from Egypt to the Euphrates River under the eternal blessing of God, could be excused for forgetting former days when his fortunes were less rosy. He earns all the more commendation for remembering the covenants he and Jonathan had sworn to each other as young adults.

What did David want to do in response to his covenant with Jonathan? (2 Sam. 9:1; 1 Sam. 20:14–16)

KINGDOM EXTRA

David's desire to show kindness to a descendant of Saul is motivated by his commitment to a previous covenant (1 Sam. 20:12–15). "Kindness" (Hebrew *chesed*) can also be translated "covenantal faithfulness," indicating that David's care for Mephibosheth is based on a commitment to a friend: David is being a promise-keeper. The Holy Spirit produces in our lives the fruit of kindness (Gal. 5:22)—an action rooted in commitment to relationship—when we are faithful to our covenant with Christ Jesus and are committed to the people around us.[5]

How did David go about tracing a survivor of Jonathan's? (2 Sam. 9:2–4)

Contrast the attitudes of David and Mephibosheth when David brought him to Jerusalem to honor him. (2 Sam. 9:5–8)

How did King David honor Mephibosheth in response to his covenant with Jonathan? (2 Sam. 9:9–13)

How could Mephibosheth's status in Israel be affected by his disability? (2 Sam. 9:3, 8, 13; see Lev. 18:16–21; Deut. 15:21)

What had been David's personal attitude toward disabled Israelites prior to caring for Mephibosheth? (2 Sam. 5:8)

 FAITH ALIVE

What kinds of disabled people sometimes find themselves separated from churches of Jesus Christ by unfriendly facilities, programs, and attitudes?

What can your church do to become more accessible to disabled people?

• In terms of facilities

• In terms of services

• In terms of acceptance

1. Joyce G. Baldwin. 1 and 2 Samuel: *An Introduction and Commentary* (Leicester, England: Inter-Varsity Press, 1988), 204.
2. *Spirit-Filled Life® Bible* (Nashville: Thomas Nelson Publishers, 1991), 592-593, "Word Wealth, 1 Chr. 16:7, thank."
3. *Hayford's Bible Handbook* (Nashville: Thomas Nelson Publishers, 1995), 101, "Surveying 1 Chronicles," note on 16:7–43.
4. *Spirit-Filled Life® Bible*, 476, map of "The Davidic Kingdom."
5. *Hayford's Bible Handbook*, 78, "Surveying 2 Samuel," note on 9:1–7.

Lesson 10/Sinning Royally
2 Samuel 10—12;
1 Chronicles 19:1—20:3

Twenty years ago Harold Fickett, a Wheaton College professor, wrote a short story about the fictitious head usher of an equally fictitious California Baptist church.[1] Those were times of recession and inflation fueled by runaway energy costs. The usher owned an appliance store that struggled due to the poor economy.

One Sunday as the head usher counted the offering after morning services, he took a one hundred dollar bill to cover a bank overdraft. During the next twelve months he embezzled seven thousand dollars, a little at a time, to keep his personal finances afloat. To his family and church friends, the head usher presented a prosperous exterior; inwardly he was suffering horrible guilt because he knew how despicably he was acting and how he was increasingly powerless to stop the downward spiral of theft and deceit.

King David of Israel was a much more powerful man around 980 B.C. than the head usher was about A.D. 1980. But his sin also started small and took on a life of its own as it grew bigger and bigger. The head usher's sin affected his family and church. However, when David, a royal figure, sinned, his sin affected an entire nation for generations.

David suffered guilt just as the head usher did. Neither escaped the searching eye of the Lord. Try as each man would to conceal his sin, Jesus' words are true: "For nothing is secret that will not be revealed, nor anything hidden that will not be known and come to light" (Luke 8:17).

BORDER SKIRMISHES

Warfare seems to have been an annual rite of spring in much of the ancient world. The name of the month March bears the name of Mars, the Roman god of war. No matter how strong or secure the reign of David would become, the spring would reveal who around the edges of his empire wanted to test his will and power to rule.

According to the following topics, describe how war broke out between Ammon and Israel.

- What David did (2 Sam. 10:1, 2; 1 Chr. 19:1, 2)

- How Hanun misinterpreted David (2 Sam. 10:3, 4; 1 Chr. 19:3, 4)

- David's response (2 Sam. 10:5; 1 Chr. 19:5)

- The next Ammonite move (2 Sam. 10:6; 1 Chr. 19:6, 7)

- The Israelite response (2 Sam. 10:7; 1 Chr. 19:8)

 BEHIND THE SCENES

Nahash of Ammon was the same king Saul had defeated at the beginning of his reign at Jabesh Gilead (1 Sam. 11:1). What kindness Nahash had shown to David is not clear. Probably he had given him some assistance during David's flight from Saul. Where Mephibosheth had accepted David's offer of kindness and was blessed (2 Sam. 9:13), Hanun rejected it by humiliating David's ambassadors and was destroyed.[2]

How did the opposing armies deploy themselves against each other? (2 Sam. 10:8–10; 1 Chr. 19:9–11)

How did Joab combine strategy and faith to attack the Ammonite-Syrian forces? (2 Sam. 10:11, 12; 1 Chr. 19:12, 13)

What was the outcome of the first battle between Israel and the Ammonites with their Syrian mercenaries? (2 Sam. 10:13, 14; 1 Chr. 19:14, 15)

What happened when the defeated Syrians tried to catch David napping after Joab and Abishai's victory over Ammon? (2 Sam. 10:15–19; 1 Chr. 19:16–19)

 FAITH ALIVE

How can we remain alert to the dangers of spiritual warfare, even when our spiritual lives are blessed and prosperous?

How can we support one another in spiritual warfare as Joab and Abishai did against the Ammonite-Syrian confederacy?

BREAKING COMMANDMENTS SIX AND SEVEN

Second Samuel 10—12 stress the use and misuse of authority. The key word that reflects power for good or ill is the verb *send* or *sent*. Scan these three chapters and underline the appearance of *send* and *sent*. How many did you find? _____ If David had not *sent* to do ill, God would not have *sent* prophecies of judgment.

What spiritual tragedy did David initiate because he stayed in the palace rather than leading his army into battle? (2 Sam. 11:1–3; 1 Chr. 20:1)

 BEHIND THE SCENES

Likely Joab had returned to Jerusalem from battling Ammon during the rainy winter months. After the final rains, the battle and the siege of the Ammonites at Rabbah (modern Amman, Jordan) was renewed. There is no reason given for David's decision to stay in Jerusalem though his place was with the armies. Had he been where he belonged, the tragedy with Bathsheba and Uriah would not have happened.[3]

KINGDOM EXTRA

One pattern of attack on our moral purity comes through the improper glance that lodges in the mind. Guard your eyes! Be warned that a lustful gaze will often lead to lustful thoughts and can result in immoral action.[4]

How did David's sin with Bathsheba follow this progression? (2 Sam. 11:2–4)

1. Lustful gaze

2. Lustful thoughts

3. Immoral action

When David discovered that Bathsheba was pregnant because of his adultery with her (2 Sam. 11:5), he made three progressively more desperate and despicable attempts to cover up his violation of the seventh commandment. Describe these three cover-up attempts.

• First cover-up (2 Sam. 11:6–11)

• Second cover-up (2 Sam. 11:12, 13)

• Third cover-up (2 Sam. 11:14–17)

 KINGDOM EXTRA

The story of David and Bathsheba provides a negative, albeit poignant, object lesson on the importance of avoiding, repenting of, and forsaking sin. Its witness is consistent with the whole counsel of God: Confess and forsake sin quickly or it will prove to be your undoing.[5]

How did the Gentile Uriah show more devotion to the Lord and the nation of Israel than David did? (2 Sam. 11:9–11)

How do you imagine Joab, the commander of the Israelite army, must have felt about sacrificing several good soldiers and breaking the sixth commandment in order to save David from embarrassment?

How did Joab and David signal to each other that the murder was done and acknowledged? (2 Sam. 11:18–25)

How did Bathsheba and David maintain an appearance of propriety? What was the Lord's assessment of what David had done? (2 Sam. 11:26, 27)

WORD WEALTH

Old Testament Hebrew used two primary words to express the idea of *husband*. Commonly a husband was identified as *baal,* which meant lord, master, even owner. If the notion of relationship was important, the noun *'ish* was used.[6] Bathsheba properly mourned as Uriah's wife ('ishah) for her husband *('ish).*

FAITH ALIVE

Why do you think that prosperity and leisure often lead to spiritual lethargy and sin?

What patterns of thought and desire tend to lead you into sin? (see James 1:13–16)

Whom do you rely on to point out to you that you are focusing on the flesh rather than God's Spirit? If you have no one to help protect you, who could fill that role for you?

FACING THE MUSIC

Anyone can sin. Anyone can be sorry when he gets caught and loses face. King Saul had done all that (1 Sam. 15:30). Perhaps the defining moment of David's reign came when God confronted him with his sin and he repented without attempt at self-justification or concern with protecting his public image.

How do you imagine Nathan the prophet may have felt when the Lord commanded him to go and confront King David with charges of adultery and murder? (2 Sam. 12:1)

In what ways was King David like the rich man in Nathan's story and Uriah the Hittite like the poor man? (2 Sam. 12:1b–4)

• Rich man/David

• Poor man/Uriah

How did David pass sentence on himself when he expressed his opinion of the selfish rich man? (2 Sam. 12:5, 6)

When Nathan said, "You are the man" (2 Sam. 12:7), what thoughts do you think flashed through David's mind? How may he have compared himself to Saul? What fears for the future may have struck him?

How did Nathan say David had despised both his anointing as king and the commandment of the Lord? (2 Sam. 12:7–9)

What consequences did Nathan prophesy David could expect to result from his sin? (2 Sam. 12:10–12)

How did David respond to Nathan's lengthy, detailed prophecy about his sin against Bathsheba and Uriah? (2 Sam. 12:13a)

What was the good news and bad news Nathan gave David in response to his confession?

• Good news (2 Sam. 12:13b)

• Bad news (2 Sam. 13:14)

 FAITH ALIVE

When we choose to sin, what blessings and promises of the Lord do we ignore and, in effect, despise?

Even though the forgiveness of God made available through the atonement provided by the blood of Jesus removes the eternal consequences of sin, what kinds of consequences in this life do our sins bear?

Once Nathan confronted David, his sin became public knowledge. How do fear and pride interfere with your readiness to admit your sins if others are to know about them?

PAYING THE PIPER

As God's anointed king over God's chosen people, David lived at a unique focal point of God's blessing and God's judgment on sin. God had forgiven David's sin that could have resulted in death (2 Sam. 12:13), but He held David accountable for the disgrace that fell on Israel and on God's name (v. 14).

What did God designate as the immediate consequence of David's sin, and how did David respond to it? (2 Sam. 12:14–16)

Do you think David's intercession for the child born to him by Uriah's wife showed unwillingness to accept God's will or confidence in his relationship to God? Why do you think so?

What troubled David's officials and servants at each of these steps of the child's illness and death?

- While David fasted and prayed (2 Sam. 12:17)

- When the child died (2 Sam. 12:18, 19)

- When David didn't mourn the child's death (2 Sam. 12:20, 21)

What do David's answers to his servants reveal concerning his attitudes about these important theological topics?

- Prayer and fasting (2 Sam. 12:22)

- The eternal destiny of infants who die (2 Sam. 12:23)

 WORD WEALTH

The Hebrew verb translated **be gracious** denotes to have compassion on someone or to bestow a favor on someone in need. Job used this word when he repeatedly and pathetically cried out to his friends, "Have pity on me" (for example, Job 19:21). **Be gracious** connotes the kind of compassion, kindness, and consideration that will cause one to refrain from further wounding an individual who is bruised and suffering.[7]

BIBLE EXTRA

Two of the psalms that David wrote in response to the crushing guilt and amazing grace that he experienced following his adultery with Bathsheba and murder of her husband Uriah are Psalms 32 and 51. Psalm 51 contrasts the deadly burden of concealed sin with the liberation of repentance and forgiveness. In Psalm 32 David praises God for His gracious forgiveness and promises to call on others to repent and turn to God for forgiveness.

What losses and hurts must he have considered when David comforted the grieving Bathsheba? (2 Sam. 12:24)

Why do you think the Lord loved Solomon (David's tenth son) and chose him as the successor to David on the throne of Israel? (2 Sam. 12:24b, 25)

While David wrestled to hide his shame and God sent Nathan the prophet to call him to repentance, Joab and the army of Israel was still laying siege to Rabbah, the royal city of Ammon. As the moment of final victory neared, what message did Joab send to King David? (2 Sam. 12:26–28; 1 Chr. 20:1b)

Describe David's part in the conquest of the Ammonite capital Rabbah. (2 Sam. 12:29–31; 1 Chr. 20:2, 3)

BEHIND THE SCENES

First and Second Chronicles were written for the exiles returning from Babylon in the fifth century B.C. To remind his readers of the blessings of God on His people when they obeyed, the Chronicler focused on godly kings and omitted incidents of sin or failure covered in the books of Samuel and

Kings. Accordingly, 1 Chronicles 20:1 skips over David's sin, repentance, forgiveness, and consequences. The Chronicler wasn't hiding the sins of David and other godly kings. He was writing a pep talk for people who had suffered through the consequences of covenant faithlessness. They knew firsthand the consequences of disobedience; they needed reminders about the blessings of obedience.

 ### FAITH ALIVE

What issue in your family life do you care about so much that God's Spirit calls to your spirit to consider urgent prayer and fasting about it?

What physical limitations (if any) must you take into account if you undertake a partial or total fast in response to your family concern?

David fasted alone because he was isolated spiritually by the awful series of sins he had engineered. Who might you ask to pray and fast with you in support of your intense concern for someone or some circumstance in your family?

1. Harold Fickett, "A Sycamore Tree," *Mrs. Sunday's Problem, and Other Stories* (Old Tappan, NJ: Fleming H. Revell Company, 1979), 15-38.
2. *Spirit-Filled Life® Bible* (Nashville: Thomas Nelson Publishers, 1991), 454, note on 2 Sam. 10:2.
3. Ibid., 455, note on 2 Sam. 11:1.
4. Ibid., 479, "Truth-in-Action through 2 Samuel."
5. Ibid., 478, "Truth-in-Action through 2 Samuel."
6. Ibid., 1259, "Word Wealth, Hos. 2:8, Baal."
7. Ibid., 1383-84, "Word Wealth, Mal. 1:9, be gracious."

Lesson 11/Reaping a Bitter Harvest
2 Samuel 13:1–19:39; 1 Chronicles 3:1–9

She sat in her pastor's office, a depressed middle-aged woman with a tale of woe. Her parents had criticized and belittled her all her life. Her husband had divorced her when the children were small. Her teenaged daughter delighted in infuriating her with defiant behavior. Her college-age son was her darling, but he came home less and less.

The pastor knew he was at a crossroads in counseling this woman. She relished telling him story after story about everyone in her life who had done her wrong. Every incident lived vividly in her memory as though they were videotapes she played over and over. She seemed to feel each person around her owed her an emotional debt.

Every attempt the pastor had made to explore the woman's responsibility for her reactions to bad experiences had been rebuffed. He had concluded since their last session that she took a perverse pleasure in wallowing in her misery. His prayer for that session was that she should recognize the harvest of bitterness that immobilized her in handling her family and in responding to God's love for her.

Nathan the prophet had predicted that King David would find that his sins of adultery and murder would echo and re-echo through his household and cause him great grief (2 Sam. 11:10–12). As the years passed, David found himself morally and spiritually paralyzed as his adult children sinned in ways similar to his great failure with Bathsheba and Uriah.

A HOUSE DIVIDED

David's second son Chileab (2 Sam. 3:3; identified as Daniel in 1 Chr. 3:1) dropped from the picture, and a struggle between first-born Amnon and third-born Absalom emerged. Behind it all was the issue of succession. Who was best positioned to succeed the aging warrior-king: the selfish, emotionally unstable Amnon, or the calculating, ambitious Absalom?

What was the relationship of Absalom and Tamar to Amnon? (2 Sam. 13:1; 1 Chr. 3:1, 2)

Who had more royal blood in his veins, Amnon or Absalom? How? (1 Chr. 3:1, 2)

What was Amnon's problem, and how did it show itself? (2 Sam. 13:1, 2, 4)

 WORD WEALTH

The Hebrew word translated **friend** (2 Sam. 13:3) occurs more than 180 times in the Old Testament. A **friend** is a companion, a neighbor, someone familiar with all one's thoughts and ways.[1] During the Israelite monarchy, there may have been an officer called the king's friend who was a close adviser to the monarch (1 Kings 4:5). Jonadab may have filled this role (2 Sam. 13:32–35).[2]

What do you learn about Amnon, in contrast to others in his family, from his rape of Tamar? (2 Sam. 13:6–11)

How did Tamar desperately reason with Amnon as she struggled against his efforts to rape her? (2 Sam. 13:12, 13)

What does it tell you about Amnon that his passion turned immediately from all-consuming desire to all-consuming hatred? (2 Sam. 13:14, 15, 17)

How significant for Tamar was the sexual assault Amnon carried out against her? (2 Sam. 13:16, 19, 20)

What kind of person was Absalom as he dealt with Tamar and got set to take revenge on Amnon? (2 Sam. 13:20–22)

Baal Hazor, where Absalom had sheep, was about fifteen miles north of Jerusalem on the highest hill in Ephraim (3,333 feet).[3] How did Absalom plot revenge against Amnon so that no one suspected what he was doing? (2 Sam. 13:23–27)

How unthinkable to everyone around Absalom was the idea of killing a royal prince? (2 Sam. 13:28–31)

What role does it seem Jonadab played in the plot to kill Amnon? (2 Sam. 13:32, 33, 35)

Where did Absalom flee for protection? (2 Sam. 13:37, 1 Chr. 3:2)

How did David mourn for Amnon and Absalom? (2 Sam. 13:36–39)

FAITH ALIVE

How did the sins of David's sons Amnon and Absalom parallel the sins of King David against Bathsheba and Uriah?

Why is it difficult to deal with our children's problems when they know we have been guilty of the same sins in the past?

How can we correct our children and help them grow spiritually in the areas of life they know have been our weaknesses in the past? How can God use our struggles to help our children?

HOW TO STEAL A KINGDOM

Absalom looked like a king. He felt that he ought to be king. He sensed that David was vulnerable. With the shrewdness of a political animal, Absalom knew when to wait without making a sound, when to insist on his way, when to tell half-truths and lies, and when and how to plot a coup.

In the narrative about King David and his son Absalom, David vacillated between administering justice or mercy. Who is the person who made David overcome his inertia? (2 Sam. 14:1, 2; 18:10–12; 19:5–7)

How did Joab convince David that it was in the best interest of the kingdom to pardon Absalom for murdering Amnon? (2 Sam. 14:1–14)

What was the wise woman's estimation of the wisdom David needed to be king over God's people (2 Sam. 14:18, 20)

How do you think King David discerned that Joab was behind the stratagem of the wise woman of Tekoa to convince him to bring Absalom home? (2 Sam. 14:18–20)

In what way did Joab's attempt to reconcile David and Absalom succeed and in what way did it fail? (2 Sam. 14:21–24)

What reasons did Absalom have for becoming increasingly vain and self-important? (2 Sam. 14:25–27)

 WORD WEALTH

Absalom was **praised** for his physical attractiveness (2 Sam. 14:25). This Hebrew verb *halal* usually is applied to God. Combined with the poetic form of His covenant name, this verb appears in the Psalms as *hallelu-Jah*. The Hebrew word for a psalm is *tehillah*, a noun made from the verb *halal*. When the people of Israel praised Absalom, they were pointing out his glories and crediting him with great honor.[4]

How did Absalom force Joab to appeal to King David for further reconciliation with him? (2 Sam. 14:28–32)

What was Absalom trying to accomplish by acting like a king on the one hand and an intimate friend on the other? (2 Sam. 15:1–6)

Once Absalom had support throughout Israel, what events set the coup d'etat in motion? (2 Sam. 15:8–12)

BEHIND THE SCENES

The reference to the passing of forty years before Absalom launched his coup (2 Sam. 15:7) can be resolved two ways. The Greek and Syriac versions of the Old Testament read "four years." Many new translations accept this variant reading. Or the biblical writer may have had in mind the passing of forty years since David had been anointed king by Samuel at Bethlehem (1 Sam. 16:13).[5]

How widespread do you think Absalom's support must have been for David to abandon Jerusalem, a fortress impregnable from without? (2 Sam. 15:13–18)

Why did Ittai, a Philistine, choose to go with David into exile? (2 Sam. 15:19–23)

Why did David want the ark and the priests to remain in Jerusalem rather than accompanying him into exile? (2 Sam. 15:24–29)

What was the spiritual, emotional, and physical state of David and the exiles as they ascended the Mount of Olives and looked back down on Jerusalem? (2 Sam. 15:30)

How did the Lord answer David's prayer concerning Ahithophel, the wisest royal adviser who had deserted to Absalom? (2 Sam. 15:31–36)

FAITH ALIVE

What was wrong or inadequate in the ways David responded to his sons when they sinned or tried to reconcile with him? (2 Sam. 13:7, 21, 25–27, 39; 14:24, 33; 15:9)

What happens in our families when we do not share openly about spiritual issues, pray together, and seek the guidance of the Spirit together?

How can Christians build families in which the kids aren't trying to take over from parents who aren't in control as they need to be?

"O MY SON, ABSALOM!"

David struggled to respond to Absalom. He loved his grown son to the point of distraction, but he could not tell him so. Absalom had done such awful things that David held him at arm's length lest he appear soft. When Absalom drove his father from the throne and took his place in Jerusalem, David vainly searched for a way to regain the throne without punishing his son.

As David fled from Jerusalem to the Jordan River, he passed through Benjamite territory where two people connected with the late King Saul's family encountered him. What did they want from King David?

• Ziba (2 Sam. 16:1–4)

• Shimei (2 Sam. 16:5–13)

WORD WEALTH

The Hebrew verb translated **cursed** (2 Sam. 16:13) literally means "to be light or insignificant." What Shimei, and others in the Old Testament who invoked formulaic curses on their foes, did was appeal to God to move David from a position of covenant blessing to the lessened or insignificant state of covenant cursing. Only God causes the state of being cursed (another Hebrew word).[6]

How did Hushai create the appearance of loyalty to Absalom without disowning David? (2 Sam. 16:15–19)

How did Ahithophel advise Absalom to demonstrate the totality of his break with his father David? (2 Sam. 16:20–23, see 12:11, 12)

How did Ahithophel advise Absalom to deal with the fleeing David and his retinue, which included David's six hundred elite fighting men? (2 Sam. 17:1–4)

How did Hushai undermine confidence in Ahithophel's advice which would have spelled doom for David who had not yet crossed the Jordan? (2 Sam. 17:5–10)

What cautious course of action did Hushai advise Absalom to adopt in dealing with David and his supporters? (2 Sam. 17:11–13)

Why did Absalom and his military leaders prefer Hushai's advice to Ahithophel's? (2 Sam. 17:4, 14)

KINGDOM EXTRA

When you face arrogant and proud opponents, pray that the Lord will confuse and frustrate their wicked and ungodly counsel. Trust that He will thwart them. Know that counsel against God's people originates from hell (no matter how wise and effective it seems) and is part of the Enemy's strategies against you.[7]

How did Hushai get word to David about the competing advice he and Ahithophel had given Absalom? (2 Sam. 17:15–22)

Why do you think Ahithophel committed suicide after his advice was rejected in favor of Hushai's? (2 Sam. 16:23; 17:23)

BEHIND THE SCENES

Ahithophel's son was named Eliam (2 Sam. 23:34). Bathsheba's father also was named Eliam (11:3). Perhaps Ahithophel was Bathsheba's grandfather. If so, he may never have forgiven David for dragging his granddaughter into a shameful situation.

What were the situations of the forces of David and Absalom as they prepared to face each other in the land of Gilead east of the Jordan? (2 Sam. 17:24–29)

How did David organize his army to face the superior numbers of Absalom's troops? (2 Sam. 18:1, 2)

What was David's personal role in the battle against Absalom? (2 Sam. 18:3–5)

How did the terrain of Gilead prove an ally to David's experienced warriors and a foe to Absalom's raw recruits? (2 Sam. 18:6–8)

Describe the conflict and emotion that surrounded the sad and ironic death of Absalom. (2 Sam. 18:9–16)

How was Absalom "memorialized"? How had he wanted to be remembered? (2 Sam. 18:17, 18)

BEHIND THE SCENES

Second Samuel 14:27 records three sons born to Absalom. Because the boys are not named, it is likely none reached manhood to figure in Absalom's proud plans for his future. Only his vanity pillar remained after a few years to mark the life of a traitor.

FAITH ALIVE

What are some of the ways that children reject their parents and break their hearts?

What is the greatest pain you have caused your parents or that your children have caused you?

What can you do from your side to apply the healing balm of God's Spirit to this family pain?

THE THRILL IS GONE

David had defeated his rival to the throne. The tribes of Israel were scrambling for the honor of being first to escort him home and swear allegiance to him. But David was sad, lonely, and looking for friends he could trust. He was tired of Joab's disregard of orders. He didn't know who to trust.

Why do you think Joab wanted a non-Israelite taking the news of Absalom's defeat and death to King David rather than Ahimaaz, the priest's son? (2 Sam. 18:19–21; see 1:1–16; 4:8–12)

What signs of anxiety do you detect in the way David waits for the runners to arrive at Mahanaim? (2 Sam. 18:22–27)

What difference existed between the news the messengers wanted to tell and the news David wanted to hear? (2 Sam. 18:28–32)

How did David mourn for his son Absalom who had tried his best to overthrow his father? (2 Sam. 18:33; 19:1, 4)

What was happening within the ranks of David's army and supporters because of the king's grief? (2 Sam. 19:2, 3)

How did Joab once again save the day for David? (2 Sam. 19:1, 5–8)

What was the political climate in Israel after Absalom's death, and how did David jump-start the movement to recall him as king? (2 Sam. 19:9–15)

Why did each of these men make sure they were in the first party that welcomed David home at Gilgal? (2 Sam. 19:16–30)

1. Shimei

2. Ziba

3. Mephibosheth

David called "the sons of Zeruiah," Joab and Abishai, "adversaries" (2 Sam. 19:22). Why do you think David was fed up with these two longtime, loyal supporters? (see v. 13)

Why did King David want to reward Barzillai the Gileadite, and why did Barzillai refuse any honors for himself? (2 Sam. 19:31–39)

 FAITH ALIVE

When in your life have you felt as though the hassles of going on were so many and the rewards so few that you did not want to go on?

How did the Lord minister to your spirit through His Spirit to give you a renewed sense of purpose and spiritual strength?

If a Christian friend asked for counsel from the Bible because family and work problems seemed overwhelming, what advice would you give?

1. *Spirit-Filled Life® Bible* (Nashville: Thomas Nelson Publishers, 1991), 906, "Word Wealth, Prov. 17:17, friend."

2. Ronald F. Youngblood, "1, 2 Samuel," *The Expositor's Bible Commentary*, Vol. 3 (Grand Rapids, MI: Zondervan Publishing House, 1992), 957.

3. Ibid., 968.

4. *Spirit-Filled Life® Bible*, 599, "Word Wealth, 1 Chr. 23:30, praise."

5. Ibid., 461, note on 2 Sam. 15:7.

6. *Theological Wordbook of the Old Testament*, Vol. II (Chicago: Moody Press, 1980), 800.

7. *Spirit-Filled Life® Bible*, 479, "Truth-in-Action through 2 Samuel."

Lesson 12/Hopes and Fears of All The Years

2 Samuel 19:40—24:25;
1 Chronicles 11:11–41;
21—29

William Shakespeare wrote historical plays based on the lives of English kings that stirred English patriotic feelings. These plays paid the bard's bills while he created more enduring dramas. King Henry V is the most attractive of Shakespeare's royal leading men. As a young monarch he led outnumbered English forces to victory in France at Agincourt. "A little touch of Harry in the night"[1] before the fateful conflict inspired the valor that will be remembered as long as there's an England.

Henry V received a legacy from his father that enabled him to succeed. Henry IV had been a good king who worried about the soundness of the legacy he would leave his son. In one scene the old king wandered his palace at Westminster late at night, thinking of his subjects slumbering in their beds while he worried about the security of the realm. "Uneasy lies the head that wears a crown," Henry soliloquized.[2]

Second Samuel ends with several chapters detailing the legacy King David was leaving his son Solomon. Some of it is sobering. Some of it is exhilarating. All of it reminds us that it is the Lord who holds the future and protects our families.

A LEGACY OF INTERNAL UNREST

The Books of 1 and 2 Samuel were probably written after Israel had divided into northern and southern kingdoms. From that perspective, events during the reigns of Saul and David that revealed long-standing tensions between the north and south hinted at the civil war that would follow the reign of Solomon.

What disagreement led to tribal division at Gilgal where David was being reinstated as king of the entire nation? (2 Sam. 19:40–43)

What final challenge to David's rule over Israel arose out of his welcome home celebration? (2 Sam. 20:1, 2)

Once David returned to Jerusalem, what decisions did he make to deal with old and new problems in his realm?

1. Concerning the concubines Absalom took as his own (2 Sam. 20:3)

2. Concerning Sheba's rebellion (2 Sam. 20:4, 5)

3. Concerning Amasa's delay (2 Sam. 20:6, 7)

How did Joab deal with the elevation of his cousin Amasa over him in David's army? (2 Sam. 20:8–13)

When Joab's army caught up with Sheba, only the clan of the Berites was supporting him militarily. How did Sheba's limited support lead to his defeat and death? (2 Sam. 20:14–22)

Compare David's administration early in his reign (2 Sam. 8:15–18) with those in position late in his reign (20:23–26) and answer these questions:

1. Who is missing from the later list? Why might this be so?

2. What is new in David's later government? Does this sound good or bad to you?

 FAITH ALIVE

How would you imagine David felt back in Jerusalem after a rebellion led by a favorite son, facing the possibility of defection by the larger portion of his kingdom, and dealing with a top general who persistently disobeyed and got away with it?

What problems are you facing inside your family, your work, your ministry, or your circle of friends?

Write a prayer in the space below imploring the Lord to give you wisdom as a peacemaker, to intervene to heal these internal divisions, and to renew this situation by His Holy Spirit.

A LEGACY OF EXTERNAL VICTORY

The progress of history in 2 Samuel ends with Sheba's rebellion. The final four chapters contain "snapshots" from various times during David's reign that picture what the realm was like at the end of his rule. David always seemed to do better when he could turn his hands and mind to dealing with foreign affairs. He was just and he was strong, whether the foreigners lived inside the land of Israel—as did the Gibeonites—or outside of it—as did the Philistines.

What was the dilemma facing Israel, and what was its cause? (2 Sam. 21:1, 2)

What did the Gibeonites demand as satisfaction for the covenant breaking of King Saul? (2 Sam. 21:3–6)

 WORD WEALTH

Make atonement translates a very important Hebrew verb that occurs more than one hundred times in the Old Testament. The primary sense of the word seems to be "to cover," as illustrated when Noah "covered" the ark inside and out with pitch (Gen. 6:14).[3] In sacrificial settings, the blood of animals atoned for the sins of the worshiper by covering them. The writer of Hebrews noted that this covering had to recur regularly; the sins were never dealt with absolutely until the blood of Christ washed them away forever (Heb. 9:12–14; 10:1–4).

How did the various participants in the macabre drama at Gibeah of Saul maintain fidelity to the covenants of their lives?

• David (2 Sam. 21:7, 8)

• The Gibeonites (2 Sam. 21:9)

• Rizpah, Saul's concubine (2 Sam. 21:10)

BEHIND THE SCENES

The reference to Michal as the wife of Adriel and mother of five of the men executed to satisfy God's anger and set right the injustice of King Saul is a scribal error. Saul's older daughter Merab was the wife of Adriel (1 Sam. 18:19). Michal bore no children (2 Sam. 6:23).

How was David moved by the fidelity of Saul's concubine Rizpah to honor the memory of Saul and his family? (2 Sam. 21:11–14)

Second Samuel 21:15–22 mentions four victories of Israelite heroes over descendants of the Philistine giant Goliath that probably occurred during the wars alluded to in chapters 5 and 8. Describe each.

2 Samuel 21:15–17

2 Samuel 21:18; 1 Chronicles 20:4

2 Samuel 21:19; 1 Chronicles 20:5

2 Samuel 21:20, 21; 1 Chronicles 20:6, 7

FAITH ALIVE

What are the "giant" problems and challenges of your life that you need the help of God's Spirit to conquer?

What examples of trusting God to kill the "giants" of life will you leave as part of your legacy to those who follow you?

A LEGACY OF SPIRIT-FILLED PRAISE

The center of the final portion of 2 Samuel consists of two songs of praise: one dating from the time of David's deliverance from King Saul (22:2–51) and the other from the days of the covenant the Lord made with David's family through Nathan the prophet (23:1–7). This beautiful poem also appears as Psalm 18. It is inconceivable that the legacy of "the sweet psalmist of Israel" (23:1) would be complete without sampling his Spirit-inspired praise.

Underline all of the titles or metaphors for God in 2 Samuel 22:2–4. What was David declaring about our heavenly Father?

What was David's experience with prayer in time of great trouble? (2 Sam. 22:5–7)

How did the Lord make Himself known to David through the world of His creation as the Deliverer? (2 Sam. 22:8–16)

How did David characterize his deliverance from destruction at the hands of the Lord? (2 Sam. 22:17–28)

 BEHIND THE SCENES

David did not consider himself sinlessly perfect. He was measuring himself against the demands of God's law in terms of how he had treated King Saul while Saul sought his life. "He had kept the ways of the Lord, refusing to kill his pursuer, and waiting for the Lord's vindication. Now that vindication had come, he could safely conclude that he was right with God."[4]

How did David describe the divine assistance God gave him when he walked in obedience to Him? (2 Sam. 22:29–37)

Describe the thoroughness of the victory David experienced through the help of the Lord. (2 Sam. 22:38–46)

What were David's conclusions based on his experience of God's wonderful blessing, protection, and prospering of his life? (2 Sam. 22:47–51)

 KINGDOM EXTRA

In this poetic song, David thanks and praises the Lord for His deliverance from all enemies and the hand of Saul (2 Sam. 22:1). Without inhibition or hesitation, he offers praise even among the Gentiles (v. 50). In the same manner, we give thanks for our deliverance through Christ (Col. 1:12, 13; 1 Thess. 1:10); and being empowered and inspired by the Spirit to witness through the words of praise (Acts 1:8; 2:11, 47; 4:21), without hesitation we offer our thanksgiving among the "Gentiles"—the unconverted—that the Spirit uses to draw them to Christ for their own deliverance.[5]

"The last words of David" (2 Sam. 23:1) function as a final testament acknowledging God's blessing on his royal family. What do these seven verses tell us about the following topics:

• David (2 Sam. 23:1, 2)

• The ideal king from David's family (2 Sam. 23:3, 4)

• The covenant God made with David's royal house (2 Sam. 23:5–7)

WORD WEALTH

The Hebrew noun translated **Spirit** (2 Sam. 23:2) occurs nearly four hundred times in the Old Testament with meanings ranging from wind to breath to human spirit to God's Spirit as in this passage. In the Old Testament the Holy Spirit is especially presented in Isaiah: God puts His Spirit upon the Messiah (42:1); He will pour out His Spirit upon Israel's descendants (44:3); Yahweh and His Spirit both send the Anointed One (48:16, a reference to the triune God); and the Spirit of God commissions and empowers the Messiah (61:1–3)[6]

FAITH ALIVE

What do you have to praise the Lord for in terms of the times He has delivered you in the past?

What do you have to praise the Lord for in terms of the blessings He is pouring out on you and those you love?

Ask the Holy Spirit to give you a song of praise based on your experience of God's deliverance and blessing. If He chooses to give you one, write its words here.

LEGACY OF HEROES

The list of heroes in 2 Samuel 23:8–39 probably recalled the glory days of the beginning of David's reign. Its parallel passage, 1 Chronicles 11:11–41, appears right after the capture of Jerusalem. The inclusion of Asahel and Uriah, who died early in 2 Samuel (2:23; 11:17), also suggests this is a list from the early days of David's kingdom. Joab is not mentioned in either list, suggesting his fame put him in a class by himself. There are thirty-six names in 2 Samuel 23:8–39. Add Joab and the total reaches thirty-seven (v. 39)

Who were the mightiest three of David's heroes? (2 Sam. 23:8–12; 1 Chr. 11:11–13)

Who were two others who distinguished themselves above "the thirty chief men"? (2 Sam. 23:18–23; 1 Chr. 11:20–25)

What feat of three of the thirty chief men attained legendary proportions and captured the spirit of this elite fighting group? (2 Sam. 23:13–17; 1 Chr. 11:15–19)

 ### FAITH ALIVE

Who do you look up to as Christians whose Spirit-filled lives are examples for you to follow?

Who among your friends or in the younger generation might look to you as an example of Spirit-filled maturity?

What "battles" do you need to win by God's grace to show the courage and endurance that marks a hero?

A LEGACY OF REPENTANCE

David's legacy of repentance is vital. He never failed to respond to a prophetic word or the conviction of the Holy Spirit. God was the true King of Israel; David merely represented Him. David never forgot that reality when faced with his sin. In time, the site David purchased from Araunah the Jebusite housed the temple Solomon built. A place of repentance became the place of atonement.

In the course of strengthening his grip on Israel, what had King David done that troubled his commander Joab and angered the Lord? (2 Sam. 24:1–4; 1 Chr. 21:2–4, 7)

How would you account for the different explanations of the spiritual motivator of David's sinful census? (2 Sam. 24:1; 1 Chr. 21:1)

Describe the military census Joab conducted and its findings. The discrepancy between the census numbers of Samuel and Chronicles may result from different ways of summarizing all the data they accumulated. (2 Sam. 24:5–9; 1 Chr. 21:5, 6)

Why do you think it was a sin for David to make a military census aimed at bolstering the size of his army? (2 Sam. 24:10; 1 Chr. 21:7, 8)

What do you think of David's selection from the three optional punishments of differing length that the Lord presented through Gad the prophet? (2 Sam. 24:11–14; 1 Chr. 21:9–13)

Describe David's attitude toward the suffering of Israel and Jerusalem caused by the plague from God. (2 Sam. 24:14–17; 1 Chr. 21:14–17)

How did David and Araunah/Ornan respond to the Lord's direction to erect a special altar on the hilltop threshing floor in response to the end of the plague? (2 Sam. 24:18–24; 1 Chr. 21:18–24)

 KINGDOM EXTRA

As with King David, unless you experience some sacrifice, you have not truly *given*. Unless your giving costs you something—something that represents a portion of your very life—then it is not a living gift and will not yield a good harvest. Our giving to the Lord must bear these three qualities.

First, it should be our *best*. When we give God our best, we are in a position to expect *His best* back into our lives. Second, we should give to God first. The very first thought in our minds after we have received something should be how we can give a portion of our harvest to the work of the Lord. Third, our giving should be *generous,* freely from our heart and without expecting anything back from the One to whom we give. As Jesus said to His disciples, "Freely you have received, freely give" (Matt. 10:8).[7]

What was the significance of the altar and the burnt offering that David offered on it at Araunah's/Ornan's threshing floor? (2 Sam. 24:25; 1 Chr. 21:28—22:1)

 BIBLE EXTRA

Read 1 Chronicles 22—29, the final chapters of the book that have no parallel in 2 Samuel. This portion of 1 Chronicles parallels part of 1 Kings 1, but its purpose in Chronicles is to reveal the depth of David's passion for the temple of the Lord that he was not permitted to build. These chapters tell how David gathered building materials, organized

priests, temple servants, and worship leaders. He gave Solomon detailed instructions and building plans. Finally 1 Chronicles records Solomon's anointing as king and David's death.

 FAITH ALIVE

Give an example of a time when you trusted in human abilities to plan and get things done rather than depending on the Lord. What happened as a result?

When have you experienced the Spirit of God convicting your heart of the wrongness of something you were doing as King David felt the Spirit's condemnation in his heart? (2 Sam. 24:10)

David's repentance paved the way for the construction of the temple on Mount Moriah (where Araunah's threshing floor was). How does our Spirit-prompted repentance result in the temple of our hearts becoming more fully God's abode?

A LEGACY OF MESSIANIC HOPE

God made a special promise to David (2 Sam. 7:8–17; 1 Chr. 17:7–14), part of which was fulfilled in the near future, part after David died, and part in the distant future. First, God promised that He would protect David from his enemies and help him bring peace to the land. Second, the Lord said that the temple would be built, but it would be built by one of David's sons, not David. As long as David's descendants obeyed God, the Lord would keep one of them as king. Third, God promised that one of David's descendants would rule Israel forever. This part of the promise looked far ahead, to the day when Jesus (the

Messiah) would rule forever. This promise to David and his descendants is still intact today.[8]

KINGDOM EXTRA

In 2 Samuel 23:1–7, David prophesied about the kind of king who would ultimately lead Israel. Only the Messiah—and not David—would fulfill this description (see also Is. 42:1–4). David acknowledged that he fell short of governing in this way (v. 5), yet he affirmed God's faithfulness to keep His covenant nonetheless. We may assure ourselves similarly that God's gifts and calling flow from His abundant grace, not from our merit (Rom. 11:29).[9]

It is no accident that the genealogies of Matthew and Luke trace the lineage of Jesus to David. Paul was doing more than being clever when he introduced his letter to the Romans by writing "concerning [God's] Son Jesus Christ our Lord, who was born of the seed of David according to the flesh, and declared to be the Son of God with power according to the Spirit of holiness, by the resurrection from the dead" (Rom. 1:3, 4). From God's covenant with David and his seed spring foundational biblical themes of the Messiah who rules over the kingdom of God. This is the enduring spiritual legacy of King David.

---

1. William Shakespeare, *King Henry V,* IV, Chorus, 47.

2. *The Second Part of King Henry IV,* III, i, 31.

3. *Spirit-Filled Life® Bible* (Nashville: Thomas Nelson Publishers, 1991), 217, "Word Wealth, Num. 15:25, make atonement."

4. Joyce G. Baldwin, *1 and 2 Samuel: An Introduction and Commentary* (Leicester, England: Inter-Varsity Press, 1988), 288.

5. *Hayford's Bible Handbook* (Nashville: Thomas Nelson Publishers, 1995), 78-79, "Surveying 2 Samuel," note on 22:47–50.

6. *Spirit-Filled Life® Bible,* 474, "Word Wealth, 2 Sam. 23:2, Spirit."

7. Ibid., 477, "Kingdom Dynamics, 2 Sam. 24:24, Give God Your Best—Then Expect His Best."

8. *The Promise: Study Edition* (Nashville: Thomas Nelson Publishers, 1995), 453, "For My Life," note on 1 Chr. 17:7–14.

9. *Hayford's Bible Handbook,* 79, "Surveying 2 Samuel," note on 23:1–7.

SPIRIT-FILLED LIFE® BIBLE DISCOVERY GUIDE SERIES

*Coming Soon

SPIRIT-FILLED LIFE® KINGDOM DYNAMICS STUDY GUIDES

OTHER SPIRIT-FILLED LIFE® STUDY RESOURCES